Second Edition

PERSONAL PRODUCTIVITY W

DOS®

Peter Lim

"real existence"

Second Edition

PERSONAL PRODUCTIVITY WITH
DOS®

KENNETH D. GORHAM

Los Angeles Mission College

Wm. C. Brown Publishers

Book Team

Editor *Kathy Shields*
Software Coordinator *Lisa Schonhoff*
Production Coordinator *Carla D. Arnold*

 Wm. C. Brown Publishers

President *G. Franklin Lewis*
Vice President, Publisher *George Wm. Bergquist*
Vice President, Operations and Production *Beverly Kolz*
National Sales Manager *Virginia S. Moffat*
Group Sales Manager *Vincent R. Di Blasi*
Vice President, Editor in Chief *Edward G. Jaffe*
Marketing Manager *Elizabeth Robbins*
Advertising Manager *Amy Schmitz*
Managing Editor, Production *Colleen A. Yonda*
Manager of Visuals and Design *Faye M. Schilling*
Production Editorial Manager *Julie A. Kennedy*
Production Editorial Manager *Ann Fuerste*
Publishing Services Manager *Karen J. Slaght*

WCB Group

President and Chief Executive Officer *Mark C. Falb*
Chairman of the Board *Wm. C. Brown*

Cover design Sailer & Cook Creative Services

Copyright © 1988, 1992 by Wm. C. Brown Publishers. All rights reserved

PC-DOS® is a registered trademark of IBM Corporation
MS-DOS® is a registered trademark of Microsoft Corporation
Lotus 1-2-3® is a registered trademark of Lotus Development Corporation
dBASE IV® is a trademark of Aston-Tate Corporation
PC-TOOLS® is a trademark of Central Point Software
Always® is a registered trademark of Funk Software

Library of Congress Catalog Card Number: 91–76586

ISBN 0-697-14076-8

No part of this publication may be reproduced, stored in a retrieval system, or transmitted, in any form or by any means, electronic, mechanical, photocopying, recording, or otherwise, without the prior written permission of the publisher.

Printed in the United States of America by Wm. C. Brown Publishers, 2460 Kerper Boulevard, Dubuque, IA 52001

10 9 8 7 6 5 4 3 2 1

Contents

Preface ix

Chapter One - The DOS Environment 1

Learning Objectives 1
DOS Defined 1
Microcomputer Systems 2
Software 2
Hardware 2
  Microprocessor Chips 3
  Memory Chips 3
  Disk Drives 4
  Adapter Cards 4
Peripherals 5
  Monitor 5
  Keyboard 6
  Printer 8
Other Peripherals 8
Terms 8
Review Questions 10
Comprehensive Problem One 11

Chapter Two - Introduction to DOS 12

Learning Objectives 12
DOS Versions 12
DOS Functions 13
DOS Commands 13
  Correcting Errors 13
  Parameters and Options 14
  DOS Command Syntax 14
Internal and External Commands 15
Booting DOS 15
  Date and Time Prompts 16
  DOS Prompt 16
  Booting Errors 16
Changing Drives 17
  Changing Drive Error 17
Commands 17
  DATE Command 17
  TIME Command 17
  VER Command 18
  CLS Command 18
  PROMPT Command 18
Printing Commands 19
  Printing Error 20
Computer Operations Tips 20
  Diskettes 20
  Diskette Drives 22

vi Contents

    Hard Disk Drives 23
    Monitors 23
    Dot Matrix Printers 23
    Laser Printers 23
Terms 24
Review Questions 25
Solving Error Messages 26
Chapter Two Tutorial 27
Comprehensive Problem Two 36

Chapter Three - Formatting Disks 38

Learning Objectives 38
FORMAT Command 38
    Tracks, Sectors, and Clusters 39
    Enhancing DOS 40
FORMAT Options 40
    FORMAT a Data Diskette 40
    FORMAT /V Option 41
    FORMAT /S Option 41
    FORMAT /4, /T:, and /N: Options 42
    Write-Protect Status 42
    Formatting Errors 42
Formatting a Hard Disk 43
VOL Command 44
LABEL Command 44
PATH Command 44
General Error Messages 45
Terms 46
Review Questions 47
Solving Error Messages 48
Chapter Three Tutorial 49
Comprehensive Problem Three 61

Chapter Four - Filenames and Directories 63

Learning Objectives 63
File names 63
DIR Command 65
    Wildcards 66
    Directory Error Messages 67
DOS Editing Keys 68
Redirection 68
Filter Commands 69
    MORE Filter 69
    SORT Filter 70
    FIND Filter 71
    Redirection Error Message 71
Terms 72
Review Questions 73
Solving Error Messages 74
Chapter Four Tutorial 75
Comprehensive Problem Four 83

Chapter Five - File Manipulation 85

Learning Objectives 85
  COPY Command 85
    COPY *.* 87
    COPY Errors 87
  XCOPY Command 87
  DISKCOPY Command 88
  DISKCOMP Command 89
  COMP Command 89
  REN Command 90
    REN Error Messages 90
  DEL Command 90
    Enhancing DOS 91
  ATTRIB Command 91
    ATTRIB Error Message 92
  CHKDSK Command 93
    Enhancing DOS 94
    CHKDSK /V (View) Option 94
  Terms 95
  Review Questions 96
  Solving Error Messages 97
  Chapter Five Tutorial 98
  Comprehensive Problem Five 105

Chapter Six - Subdirectory System 108

Learning Objectives 108
Root Directory 108
Subdirectory System 108
  Subdirectories 109
  Subdirectories and Files 109
  Current Directory 109
  Directory Path 110
  Full Pathname 110
  Subdirectories within Subdirectories 110
Subdirectory Commands 111
  MD Command 111
  MD Error Message 111
  CD Command 112
  CD Error Message 113
  RD Command 113
  RD Error Message 114
  PATH Command 114
  Copying Files to Subdirectories 115
  XCOPY /S and /E Options 116
  TREE Command 116
  Enhancing DOS 117
  ATTRIB /S Option 117
Terms 118
Review Questions 119
Solving Error Messages 120
Chapter Six Tutorial 121

Comprehensive Problem Six 130

Chapter Seven - Batch Files 132

Learning Objectives 132
Batch Files 132
  Stopping a Batch File 132
  Storing Batch Files 133
  Batch File Filenames 133
Creating Batch Files 133
  AUTOEXEC.BAT File 133
  COPY CON: 134
EDLIN 134
  Creating Batch Files With EDLIN 135
  Editing an Existing File 138
  Backup Files 139
  Edlin Error Message 139
TYPE Command 139
REM Subcommand 140
Terms 140
Review Questions 141
Chapter Seven Tutorial 142
Comprehensive Problem Seven 149

Chapter Eight - Subcommands and Hard Disk Commands 150

Learning Objectives 150
Subcommands 150
  ECHO Subcommand 151
  Replaceable Parameters 151
  GOTO Subcommand 152
  Documenting Batch Files 152
Hard Disk Commands 153
  PARK Command 153
  FDISK Command 154
Backing Up Hard Disks 154
  BACKUP Command 154
  RESTORE Command 157
Updating DOS 158
  SYS Command 158
  REPLACE Command 158
  Terms 159
  Comprehensive Problem Eight 159
Review Questions 160

Appendix A - Memory Types and CONFIG.SYS File 161
Appendix B - DOS Version 4 167
Appendix C - Glossary 170
Appendix D - Command Summary 174
Appendix E - Error Message Summary 181
Appendix F - Keyboard Diagrams 188
Index 189

Preface

This text, an updated and improved version of *Personal Productivity with DOS*, covers beginning and intermediate DOS commands. The second edition covers many more commands and command options and updates the coverage through DOS Version 4. The text has been carefully constructed so that it can be used with Version 2.0 through Version 4.01. A new chapter has been added which covers the batch file subcommands (ECHO, REM, PAUSE, and GOTO) and hard disk commands (FDISK, PARK, BACKUP, RESTORE, SYS, and REPLACE). Common DOS error messages are displayed in the text and the solution to these errors is explained. Weaknesses of DOS are discussed, and third-party software solutions to these shortcomings are recommended. This text combines a complete discussion of the material followed by tutorial exercises that teach the student how use DOS on the microcomputer. A series of comprehensive problems are used to have the student apply the material learned in each chapter to solve real-world DOS problems. This text can be used with either MS-DOS or PC-DOS. This text was designed for the IBM microcomputer or compatible with two diskette drives, or a hard drive and one diskette drive. This text has been designed to be used in a five-to ten-week course. If the course covers two to four weeks, the text *Personal Productivity with DOS Primer* could be used.

Tutorial Lessons and Chapter Learning Aids

The text assumes no prior knowledge by the students. The tutorial exercises have been constructed to lead the students, step by step, through the most common commands of DOS. Each tutorial includes numerous screen-display checkpoints. The students will be able to check their work against the screen displays to make sure that they have followed the steps correctly. The tutorials are constructed so that students may progress at their own pace and may repeat any part of the tutorial as many times as is necessary to learn the material. A separate set of tutorials have been created for floppy disk systems (two floppy disks and no hard disk) and hard disk computers (a hard disk and one floppy disk). There are true/false, fill-in, and discussion questions at the end of each chapter. Most chapters have an error-solving section where the student, presented with several DOS error messages, must tell how to solve the errors. Eight comprehensive problems that the student must work out on the computer are included in the text.

Appendices

Appendix A discusses expanded and extended memory and has complete coverage of the CONFIG.SYS file. Appendix B discusses the new features introduced in Version 4 of DOS. A glossary of terms is found in Appendix C. Appendix D contains a command summary that divides commands into functional areas. Appendix E includes a complete error-message summary which presents common DOS error messages and their solutions. The error messages are organized by the type of command that would generate them. The last page of Appendix E supplies a set of hardware error messages. Appendix E has diagrams of the original and enhanced keyboard. The instructor's manual and disk include a test bank with more than 250 questions. No special student disk is necessary for this text. This text is part of a series of microcomputer applications texts that includes the following titles:

Personal Productivity with DOS Primer, Second Edition.
Personal Productivity with DOS, Second Edition.
Personal Productivity with Lotus 1-2-3, Third Edition.
Personal Productivity with Advanced Lotus 1-2-3.
Personal Productivity with WordPerfect.
Personal Productivity with dBase III.

The DOS Environment

Chapter 1

Learning Objectives

After completing chapter one you will be able to:

```
 1. Define hardware and software.
 2. Define the components of the systems unit.
 3. Define the difference between ROM and RAM.
 4. Differentiate between temporary and permanent memory.
 5. Define the different types of disk drives.
 6. Define the function of adapter cards.
 7. Define the different types of display adapter cards.
 8. Define the different parts of the keyboard.
 9. Define the different types of printers.
10. Define the use of tape backup, mouse, and modem devices.
```

DOS Defined

This text assumes that you are using an operating systems program called PC-DOS Version 3.3 or MS-DOS Version 3.3. If you are using another version of DOS, your screen displays will be slightly different. Important differences in earlier versions of DOS and features introduced in Version 4 are also discussed. When keys are used in this text they will be enclosed in angle brackets (for example, <ENTER>). Since PC-DOS and MS-DOS are virtually identical, the program will be called **DOS** (an acronym for Disk Operating System). A **computer program** is a set of commands that instructs a computer to perform a task. The **operating system program** is a program that manages the computer system. Computer information is stored on storage media called a **disk**. DOS creates a storage facility on disk called a **file** to store groups of related information. For example, these files can be word processing documents or spreadsheets. An important function of DOS is to control the storage of files on disk. DOS is also used to manage printers and other devices (mouse, modem, and so on). DOS is also used by applications programs such as word processors or spreadsheets to store files on disk and retrieve files from disk.

DOS is a command-driven operating system. You must enter DOS commands to make DOS perform its operations. Other operating systems offer menus or pictures to show the available options. You may wonder why DOS is so important to understand, especially if you plan on only using application programs. It is important because any application program, such as Lotus 1-2-3, must be accessed through DOS. You will also be more efficient in your interaction with application programs when you are familiar with DOS. You can use DOS to configure your system so that application programs will operate at maximum efficiency. DOS can automate procedures so that you can efficiently manage your disk files and move smoothly from one application program to another.

Microcomputer Systems

A **system** is a group of elements that, when properly combined, produces a result. A **microcomputer system** is a collection of hardware components that work together. An operating system is a group of programs that work with the microcomputer system to produce results. Before DOS can be explored, an understanding of what constitutes a typical microcomputer system must be achieved. This knowledge will also assist students if they purchase their own computer. A microcomputer system consists of two major items: software and hardware. **Software** is the programs that tell the machinery what to do. The DOS program is an example of a piece of software. **Hardware** is the tangible, physical machinery.

Software

Software consists of programs or lists of instructions to the computer. Software that a microcomputer user will encounter can be divided into three basic categories: operating systems programs, applications programs, and utility programs. Operating systems programs are programs that are used to start the computer, work with applications software, and store data. The DOS program is an example of a operating systems program. **Applications programs** are programs that are used to accomplish a particular function. The most popular type of applications software are word processing programs such as WordPerfect which are used to create letters and other documents, spreadsheet programs such as Lotus 1-2-3 which are used for budgeting and financial analysis, and database management programs such as dBase IV which is used to create electronic filing systems. **Utility Programs** are programs that when added to operating systems or applications software, provide additional flexibility and ease of use. There are some utility programs provided with DOS (for example, EDLIN, a text editor) and you can buy utility programs from other software companies that make DOS easier to use. Some utility programs may be added to applications software. For example, you may buy additional utilities for your spreadsheet software that will enhance the graphics, enhance the printing, and make the spreadsheet program easier to use. Some examples of popular utility programs used to enhance DOS are PC-TOOLS and Xtree. Allways and Freelance are examples of popular utility programs that enhance the Lotus 1-2-3 application program.

Hardware

A **microcomputer**, an electronic device controlled by instructions stored within its memory, allows data to be entered, processed, outputted, and stored. **Data** is the words or numbers processed by the microcomputer to create useful information. Microcomputers perform four basic functions: input, processing, storage, and output. All pieces of hardware perform at least one of these functions and some hardware devices perform two of these functions. Processing involves changing or manipulating data to produce usable information. The **microprocessor chip** is the hardware device that does the processing. Data must be input to the computer so that it can be processed. Data is typically inputted from the **keyboard** or a **disk drive**. Information can be outputted on a device called a **monitor** that looks like a TV screen or outputted as a printed document by a device called a **printer**. Information is stored by writing it to a disk so that the information can be recalled in the future. The hardware units that are typically part of a microcomputer system are the **systems unit** which contains the microprocessor chip, RAM and ROM memory chips, disk drives, and adapter cards. The input devices may include the keyboard, which is used to enter data and commands and a **mouse**, which may be used in place of or in addition to a keyboard to enter commands. Storage devices include the disk drive which is used to store data and programs and **tape backup units** which are used to backup information stored on disk. Output devices include the monitor which displays output from the microcomputer and also displays data and commands as they are entered by the user and the printer, which provides hard copy (printed) output.

Microprocessor Chips

The type of microprocessor chip installed in the systems unit determines the type of systems unit. The microprocessor chip drives the rest of the computer system. There are currently five different types of microprocessors. Each generation of microprocessor is faster than the one that preceded it. The original IBM PC, introduced in 1981, used an 8088 microprocessor. The 80286 chip was first introduced in 1984. The 80386 chip began appearing in 1987 and is currently the most popular type of chip used. The 80486 chip is the most advanced chip on the market and a small percentage of microcomputers use this chip. The following chart summarizes the types of microcomputers:

Type	Word Size	MHz	Example
8088	16-bit word/8-bit data path	4.77	IBM PC/XT
8086	16-bit word/16-bit data path	12	IBM PS/2 Model 30
80286	32-bit word/16-bit data path	33	IBM AT
80386	32-bit word/32-bit data path	33	IBM PS/2 Model 50 Compaq Deskpro 386
80486	32-bit word/32-bit data path	50	IBM PS/2 Model 80 Compaq SystemPro

Microcomputer types

Computer chips, including microprocessor chips, store information by assigning a value of either 0 or 1 to the smallest unit of storage, a binary digit or a **bit**. Eight of these bits grouped together forms a **byte**. It takes one byte to store each character in a computer chip. A character is a number (0-9), a letter (A-Z), or a special character such as a question mark, a dollar sign and so on. When bytes are grouped together (always in multiples of 2), the groups are called **words**. A 16-bit word represents two characters and a 32-bit word represents four characters. The **word size** of a microprocessor determines how much data can be processed at one time. As the word size increases more data can be processed with each pass and the computer operates faster. The word size used within the microprocessor and the word size for input/output can differ as in the case of the 8088 chip (16-bit within the microprocessor, 8-bit input/output path). The word size used for input/output determines how fast information can be inputted to the microprocessor and outputted from the microprocessor. A clock is used in each microprocessor to control how fast it operates. A **megahertz (MHz)** is a unit used to measure how fast the clock runs. A megahertz is one million cycles per second. The faster the clock is driven, the faster the microcomputer. For example, you can purchase 80386 computers that run at 16 megahertz or 33 megahertz.

Memory Chips

The systems unit contains two types of memory chips, **ROM (Read Only Memory)** and **RAM (Random Access Memory)**. Microcomputers typically have a small amount of ROM and a large amount of RAM. Both types of memory are stored on a physical unit called a **memory chip**. ROM is called Read Only Memory because you cannot write into this memory, you can only read from this memory. ROM contains programs that have been permanently encoded into ROM chips and are used when the computer is turned on. One of the ROM programs allows the computer to start itself, the equivalent of a starter on a car. Another ROM program monitors the keyboard for activity and sends the keystrokes to DOS for analysis. ROM memory is permanent because it is not erased when you turn the computer off. RAM is called random access memory because you both read from and write to this memory. RAM is known as temporary memory because it is erased when the computer is turned off. When the microcomputer is powered on, programs (including DOS) are loaded into RAM and data is manipulated within RAM. When you create a letter with your word processing program or create a budget with your spreadsheet program this information is manipulated in RAM.

4 The DOS Environment

Since RAM will be erased when the microcomputer is turned off, you must, at some point, save your letter or spreadsheet to disk memory. The amount of RAM is usually at least 256,000 characters but many users add more RAM to their computers. The amount of RAM needed in a microcomputer is determined by the requirements of the software used. For example, Lotus 1-2-3 Version 2.2 requires 256,000 characters of RAM while WordPerfect Version 5.1 requires 512,000 characters of RAM. The size of RAM is measured in **kilobytes** or **megabytes**. One kilobyte (**KB**) of RAM actually contains 1,024 bytes but it is usually rounded to 1,000 bytes. One megabyte (**MB**) of RAM actually contains 1,048,576 bytes but is usually rounded to 1,000,000 bytes. Since one byte can store one character, a microcomputer with 256KB of RAM can store about 256,000 characters and a microcomputer with 1MB of RAM can store about 1,000,000 characters.

Disk Drives

The disk drives are the microcomputer's permanent memory device. When the microcomputer is turned off, RAM is erased. Turning the computer off has no effect on disk memory. There are two types of disk drives, floppy drives and hard drives. Floppy drives are external drives and the user has to insert a disk (also called a diskette) into the floppy disk drive. The hard drive (also called a fixed disk) is internal (hidden inside the systems unit). There are two types of floppy drives, a drive that uses a 5.25-inch-diameter disk and a drive that uses a 3.5-inch-diameter disk. The 5.25-inch drive is the original type of drive. The 3.5-inch drive has become the most popular type of drive because the diskette used is more durable than a 5.25-inch diskette. The 3.5-inch diskette is stored within a rigid case while the 5.25-inch diskette is stored within a flexible case. Version 3.2 of DOS supports 3.5-inch diskettes; earlier versions do not. The terms byte, kilobyte, and megabyte are also used to define the amount of disk storage. Both types of diskettes can have data stored on them using different densities.

Density is a measure of the number of magnetic spots recorded in a one-inch area on the diskette. The original 5.25-inch double-density diskette could store about 360KB bytes of data. A high-density (also called a quad-density) diskette can store more than one megabyte of data. Both the 3.5-inch and 5.25-inch diskettes can be purchased in either double-density or high-density formats. If you have one floppy drive it is known as the A drive. If you have two floppy drives they are known as the A and B drives. Unlike the floppy diskette a hard drive is permanently installed in the microcomputer and cannot be removed by the user. Hard drives can usually store at least 10MB of data and larger hard drives can store as much as 600MB of data. Hard drives are at least twenty times faster than floppy drives. The hard drive is named the C drive and if you have multiple hard drives you may also have a D or E drive and so on. A system that has a hard drive must have at least one floppy drive because software programs that are purchased must be initially loaded onto the hard disk from a floppy drive, The floppy drive can also be used to backup the hard drive and to transfer data to other microcomputers.

Adapter Cards

Adapter cards installed inside the systems unit, customize the microcomputer to your individual specifications. Just as some cars may have air conditioning and power windows and other cars have no air conditioning and manual windows, microcomputers can be configured with a variety of options. These options require that an adapter card be installed to connect the option to the systems unit. The adapter card is installed in an **expansion slot** that is mounted on a printed circuit board called the **motherboard** that forms the bottom of the systems unit. The microprocessor, RAM, and ROM are also plugged into the motherboard. The expansion slots are all connected to a common communications channel called a **bus**. The first systems had an 8-bit bus but modern systems have either a 16-bit or 32-bit bus. The wider the bus the faster data can be transferred. Microcomputers have from three to ten expansion slots depending upon the type of system. The number of expansion slots determines how many options can be added to a microcomputer. Most microcomputers have two adapter cards as standard equipment. You must have a disk-drive controller card to connect your diskette or hard disk to the systems unit. You must also have a display card to connect your monitor to the systems unit. Other types of adaptor cards may include a memory card containing additional RAM and a printer interface card to connect a printer to the systems unit. The adapter cards often have **ports** on the back of the card that can be seen at the back of the microcomputer. These ports are used to connect hardware devices to the systems unit.

Since hardware devices are either parallel or serial devices, ports are also either parallel or serial. **A serial port** transfers data one bit at a time while a **parallel port** transfers data eight bits at a time. You must connect a parallel device with a parallel port and a serial device with a serial port. For example, the IBM monochrome display card comes with a parallel printer port. A parallel cable would be used to connect a parallel printer with the parallel printer port. Serial devices include the mouse and the modem while virtually all other devices are parallel devices.

Peripherals

Every piece of hardware that is connected to the systems unit with an adapter card or a cable is known as a peripheral. Common peripherals include the keyboard, monitor, printer, and disk drive.

Monitor

A monitor is a display screen that allows the user to see what is being keyed into RAM or displayed from RAM. Monitors typically display eighty characters horizontally and twenty-five lines vertically on the screen. A flashing dash called a cursor marks your current position on the screen. If you move the cursor to the top or the bottom of the screen, data must be scrolled on and off the screen because only twenty-five lines by eighty characters can be displayed at one time. There are two types of monitors: monochrome (single color) and color. A monochrome monitor displays green, amber, or white characters on a black background. Color monitors can display multiple colors. The quality of the monitor and the type of display adapter card connected to the monitor determines the resolution or clarity of the display. The resolution of display adapter cards is primarily determined by the amount of picture elements or **pixels** displayed by the card. A pixel is an individual point on the screen used to create each character. The pixel rate is measured horizontally and vertically. For example, a 320 x 200 pixel monitor displays 320 horizontal pixels by 200 vertical pixels.

Another element that determines the resolution of the picture is the horizontal scanning frequency (the rate at which one line is draw across the width of the screen) and the **vertical scanning frequency** (VSF), also called the refresh or frame rate (the rate at which a complete screen is filled with an image). The standard vertical scanning frequency is 60Hz (the screen is redrawn 60 times per second). A few monitors and display cards support a 72Hz refresh rate which significantly reduces eye strain. The type of scanning supported by the monitor and the display card also determines the resolution. Most monitors use **interlaced scanning** which means that the monitor takes two passes to create an image instead of one, causing screen flicker. A few monitors and display cards support **noninterlaced scanning** which means the image is created in only one pass. Next to resolution, **dot pitch** is the most important factor in determining the apparent sharpness of a screen. Dot pitch is the distance between the pixels. All other things being equal, the smaller the dot pitch (expressed in millimeters), the sharper the image. The following table summarizes the different types of display adapter cards:

Type	Pixels	Graphics/Color Pallette
MDA	750 x 350	Monochrome without graphics.
Hercules	750 x 348	Monochrome with graphics.
CGA	320 x 200	Color (4 colors with pallette of 16).
EGA	640 x 350	Color (16 colors with pallette of 64).
VGA	640 x 480	Color (16 colors with pallette of 256).
Super VGA	800 x 600	Color (16 colors with pallette of 256).

Display Adapter Cards

6 The DOS Environment

The original Monochrome Display Adapter (MDA) card had high resolution of 750 x 350 but the original Color Graphics Adapter (CGA) card displayed color graphics (4 colors out of a pallette of 16) at a low resolution of 320 x 200. The Enhanced Graphics Adapter (EGA) card, introduced in 1984, displayed color (16 colors out of a pallette of 64) with high resolution (640 x 350). The Video Graphics Array (VGA) card, currently the most popular type of display card, is used for both high resolution monochrome and color monitors and has a resolution of 640 x 480. The super VGA display card, offering a resolution of 800 x 600, can display 16 colors out of a pallette of 256. Some super VGA cards have a resolution of 1024 x 768 and can display 256 colors.

Keyboard

The keyboard is used by the operator to enter commands and data to the computer system. When a key is pressed, a signal flows from the keyboard, through a cable, into memory, where a code representing the character keyed in is stored. The keys are typematic, which means that if you hold them down for a fraction of a second the keyboard will continue to type the same character until you release the key. You will use this feature when you wish to repetitively enter the same character. Since the keyboard is electronic and not mechanical, a very light touch is required. All keyboards have a **keyboard buffer**, or memory unit that stores keystrokes. You may sometimes have to wait for a DOS to catch up with you, particularly if you're a fast typist. Learn to adjust your typing speed to the program. Accurate typing is more important than speed. As you gain knowledge of the DOS commands, your speed will naturally increase. The **original keyboard**, released in 1981, had about eighty keys. This keyboard has ten programmable **function keys**. DOS has programmed some of the function keys to simplify the entry of DOS commands. The IBM AT keyboard released in 1984 repositioned some keys and enlarged other keys. In addition, LED indicators were added to the AT keyboard to indicate the status of some of the **toggle** keys. A toggle key is like a light switch; it may be either on or off. For example, if the <CAPS LOCK> key is toggled on, all alphabetic characters will be capitalized. The **cursor control keys** are used to change the position of the cursor on the screen and were included as part of the **numeric keypad** portion of the keyboard. The <NUM LOCK> toggle key had to be used to toggle the original keyboard and AT keyboard to either cursor control mode or numeric keypad mode.

The **enhanced keyboard** released in 1986 has more than one hundred keys. Appendix F has diagrams of the original and enhanced keyboards. The enhanced keyboard added a separate set of cursor control keys so that the <NUM LOCK> key does not have to be used to toggle the numeric keypad from numeric mode to the cursor control mode. This keyboard also repositioned the function keys from the left side of the keyboard to the top of the keyboard and added two new function keys. The enhanced keyboard also has LED indicators to display the status of the toggle keys. Both keyboards are divided into five sections: the **alphabetic keyboard** (found in the center of the keyboard), the **control keys** (found to the left and to the right of the alphabetic keyboard), the **function keys** (found on the left-hand side of the original keyboard or on the top of the enhanced keyboard), the **numeric keypad** (found on the right-hand side of the keyboard), the **cursor control keys** (found on the enhanced keyboard between the alphabetic keyboard and the numeric keypad).

The alphabetic keyboard contains the normal typewriter keys, alphabetic keys (A-Z), number keys (0-9), and special character keys. These keys are all cream colored. The function keys are numbered F1 through F10 on the original keyboard and F1 through F12 on the enhanced keyboard. The control keys are found to the left and to the right of the alphabetic keyboard. These keys are all dark gray in color and include the <ESC>, <CTRL>, <SHIFT>, <ALT>, <BACKSPACE>, <ENTER>, <CAPS LOCK>, <NUM LOCK>, <SCROLL LOCK>, <BREAK>, <PRTSC>, <PRINT SCREEN>, <PAUSE>, <DEL>, and <INS> keys. Control keys are often used in a key sequence. To enter a key sequence you first press and hold one key and then tap the other key. Key sequences will always be shown with the keys separated by a hyphen. An example of a key sequence is the <SHIFT-PRTSC> sequence which is used to print the current screen. The following table summarizes the differences in control keys between the original and enhanced keyboards:

Key	Original	Enhanced
ENTER	Labeled with a left arrow with an upstroke on the end.	Labeled Enter.
BACKSPACE	Labeled with a left arrow.	Labeled Backspace.
BREAK	On <SCROLL LOCK> key.	On <PAUSE> key.
PRTSC	<SHIFT-PRTSC> prints screen.	<PRINT SCREEN> prints screen.
PAUSE	<CTRL-S> pauses screen.	<PAUSE> pauses screen.
NUM LOCK	Toggle between cursor control and numeric keypad.	Not used as a toggle because of separate cursor keys.

Original vs. enhanced keyboard

The control keys used on the enhanced keyboard are summarized by the following table:

Key	Function
ENTER	Pressed to send commands to DOS.
BACKSPACE	Deletes character to left of cursor.
ESC (Escape)	Pressed to cancel operating DOS commands.
CTRL (Control)	Always used in combination with another key.
ALT (Alternate)	Always used in combination with another key.
SHIFT	Always used in combination with another key. Press and hold <CTRL>, <ALT>, or <SHIFT> and then tap the other key or keys.
BREAK	<CTRL-BREAK> sequence used to cancel commands.
CAPS LOCK	When toggled on, capitalizes alpha characters.
PRINT SCREEN	Used to print the screen.
PAUSE	Pauses screen.
DEL (Delete)	Deletes the character at the cursor location.
INS (Insert)	Used to insert characters at the cursor location in a DOS command.

Control keys

8 The DOS Environment

Printer

The printer is the hard-copy output device of the microcomputer. There are two types of printers: letter quality and non-letter quality. A letter-quality printer produces a solid character that looks like it was produced on a typewriter. The original letter-quality printer was the **daisy wheel printer** which produced letter-quality output but at a very slow speed. The daisy wheel has been supplanted by the **laser printer** which can produce letter-quality output six times faster than the daisy wheel. The laser printer prints both text and graphics while the daisy wheel was limited to text. The **ink jet printer** is a slightly less expensive alternative to the laser printer. The ink jet printer prints both text and graphics but the quality of the output is just below the quality of the output of a laser printer. The non-letter-quality printer is typified by the **dot matrix printer** which produces a character by printing a series of tiny dots which map out the character. The dot matrix is the least expensive type of printer selling for as little as $150.00. The latest models can produce near-letter-quality output by re-printing each character and adding additional dots to fill in the character. The normal mode of a dot matrix printer is called draft mode and is the fastest mode. Near-letter-quality printing cuts the print speed to about half the normal draft speed.

Other Peripherals

There are some other less common devices that may be part of your microcomputer system. These devices include mouse devices, modems, and tape backup units. A mouse is used in place of or in addition to a keyboard. You use the mouse to position the cursor to a point on the screen and then press buttons on the mouse to select a command rather than typing in the command from the keyboard. Mouse devices are particularly popular with graphical software. A **modem** is used to communicate with another computer over telephone lines. Information can be sent by modem from one computer to another. A modem is used to connect a microcomputer to other microcomputers or to larger computers. A modem can be an external device connected to the systems unit by a cable or it can be an internal device mounted on an adapter card with is plugged into an expansion slot. Tape backup units are used to backup the information stored on the hard disk. You can backup your hard disk to floppy disks, but it would take many floppy disks. A tape backup device will allow you to backup an entire hard disk onto one tape cassette. If the hard disk fails, the information can be restored from the tape cassette.

Terms

Adapter cards (4)
Alphabetic keyboard (6)
Applications programs (2)
Bit (3)
Bus (4)
Byte (3)
Computer program (1)
Control keys (6)
Cursor (5)
Cursor control keys (6)
Daisy wheel printer (7)
Data (2)
Density (4)
Disk drive (2)
Dot matrix printer (8)
Dot pitch (5)
Enhanced keyboard (6)
Expansion slot (4)
Function keys (6)

Hardware (2)
Ink jet printer (7)
Interlaced scanning (5)
Keyboard (2)
Keyboard Buffer (6)
Kilobytes (KB) (4)
Laser printer (7)
Megabytes (MB) (4)
Megahertz (MHz) (3)
Memory chip (3)
Microcomputer (2)
Microcomputer system (2)
Microprocessor chip (2)
Modem (8)
Monitor (2)
Motherboard (4)
Mouse (2)
Noninterlaced scanning (5)
Numeric keypad (6)
Operating system program (1)
Original keyboard (6)
Parallel port (5)
Peripheral (5)
Pixels (5)
Ports (4)
Printer (2)
RAM (3)
ROM (3)
Serial port (5)
Software (2)
System (2)
Systems unit (2)
Tape backup units (2)
Toggle (6)
Utility Programs (2)
Vertical scanning frequency (VSF) (5)
Word size (3)
Words (3)

10 The DOS Environment

Review Questions

Name_____

Mastery Self-Quiz True/False

Answer T for true or F for false

1.___ MS-DOS and PC-DOS are completely different operating systems.
2.___ Hardware is the programs that drive the computer.
3.___ RAM is known as read-only memory.
4.___ Disk drives form the temporary memory of the computer.
5.___ Eight bits forms a byte.
6.___ A megahertz is one million cycles per second.
7.___ A kilobyte is about 1,000,000 bytes.
8.___ A computer with an 8-bit word size is faster than a one with a 16-bit word size.
9.___ A serial port transfers data eight bits at a time.
10.___ Lotus 1-2-3 is an example of an applications program.

Mastery Self-Quiz Fill-in

1. _____ is the tangible, physical machinery.
2. The _____ is used to backup data stored on disk.
3. _____ stands for Read Only Memory.
4. A _____ is a million bytes.
5. Adapter cards are plugged into _____.
6. A _____ transfers data one bit at a time.
7. A _____ is an individual point on the screen used to create each character.
8. The _____ are assigned commands by DOS.
9. The _____ key is used to send commands to DOS.
10. The daisy wheel printer has been replaced by the _____.

Discussion Questions

1. Identify the hardware units contained within the system unit.

2. Discuss the difference between RAM and ROM.

3. Identify and give examples of the three different types of software.

Comprehensive Problem One

You must be familiar with the type of hardware that is found in your computer center. Check with your instructor or go to the computer center to fill out the following survey.

Microprocessors: What type of microprocessors are used in the computer center?

```
8088       Yes _____    No _____
80286      Yes _____    No _____
80386      Yes _____    No _____
80486      Yes _____    No _____
```

What type of floppy disk drives are used in the computer center?

```
5.25-inch double-density    Yes _____    No _____
5.25-inch high-density      Yes _____    No _____
3.50-inch double-density    Yes _____    No _____
3.50-inch high-density      Yes _____    No _____
```

What types of microcomputer systems are used in the computer center?

```
Floppy systems (two floppies and no hard disk)   Yes ___   No ___
Hard disk systems (one floppy and a hard disk)   Yes ___   No ___
```

What type of monitors are used in the computer center?

```
Monochrome    Yes _____    No _____
Color         Yes _____    No _____
```

What type of display cards are used in the computer center?

```
CGA    Yes _____    No _____
EGA    Yes _____    No _____
VGA    Yes _____    No _____
```

What type of printers are used in the computer center?

```
Ink Jet       Yes _____    No _____
Laser         Yes _____    No _____
Dot Matrix    Yes _____    No _____
```

Introduction to DOS

Chapter 2

Learning Objectives

After completing chapter two you will be able to:

```
1. Boot the microcomputer.
2. Change the default drive.
3. Use DATE to change the system date.
4. Use TIME to change the system time.
5. Use VER to check the version of DOS loaded in RAM.
6. Use CLS command to clear the screen.
7. Use PROMPT command to create a custom prompt.
8. Print the current screen from DOS.
```

DOS Versions

The following table summarizes the different versions of DOS:

DOS Version	Reason for Change
1.0	Original version.
2.0	Adds support for hard disk drives.
2.1	Adds support for international symbols.
3.0	Adds support for high-density 5.25-inch drives.
3.1	Adds support for networking computers.
3.2	Adds support for 3.5-inch drives.
3.3	Adds support IBM PS/2 series.
4.0	Menu-driven interface.
4.1	Corrected errors in Version 4.0.

DOS Versions

There have been four major versions of DOS: 1.0, 2.0, 3.0, and 4.0. Versions are numbered X.X. If the version increases a whole number (from 2.0 to 3.0) it represents a major change in DOS. If the version increases by the number after the decimal (3.0 to 3.1) it represents a minor change in DOS. This text uses Version 3.3 for all examples, but all of the examples will work on previous versions of DOS, with few exceptions, starting with Version 2.0. Version 4 is discussed in Appendix B.

DOS Functions

DOS has four major functions:

```
1. Control the input and output operations of the microcomputer.
2. Accept, interpret, and execute commands entered by the user.
3. File management (copy, rename, and erase files).
4. Microcomputer system configuration using the CONFIG.SYS file.
```

All applications programs need to perform input operations (receive input from keyboard or disk) and perform output operations (store files on disk and print output). Without DOS, each application program would have to create the instructions necessary to do these tasks. The DOS system contains two **DOS system files** that perform the input/output operations for DOS and application programs. These files are called **MSDOS.SYS** and **IO.SYS** in the MS-DOS system (in the PC-DOS system they are called **IBMDOS.COM** and **IBMBIO.COM**). These files are called **hidden files** because they are not shown when DOS lists the contents of a disk. The MSDOS.SYS program receives all requests for DOS services and formats them so that they can be sent to the IO.SYS program for processing. The IO.SYS (Basic Input/Output) file contains additions and corrections to the basic I/O system routines (BIOS) that are encoded in each system's ROM chips. These routines handle the input and output between the microprocessor and peripheral devices such as a disk or a printer. The third DOS system file, **COMMAND.COM**, is called the **DOS command processor** and is the interface between the user and DOS. The DOS command processor accepts, interprets, and executes DOS commands entered by the user. A **DOS command** is a character-string specification that references the name of a DOS program. Each DOS command specifies a particular DOS program that must be used to perform a task. The file management ability of DOS allows the user to manage disk files that are created. A special file called **CONFIG.SYS** can be created and changed by the user to configure their microcomputer system so that applications programs can operate at their optimum level of efficiency.

DOS Commands

You communicate with DOS by typing a DOS command and then pressing <ENTER> to send the command to DOS. Commands will be shown in uppercase characters in this text but they can be entered in uppercase or lowercase characters, or a mixture of uppercase and lowercase characters. DOS commands are programs that DOS runs to perform specific tasks. This DOS command clears the display screen and places the cursor in the upper left-most position on the screen:

```
CLS
```

Correcting Errors

You are typing a DOS command and you press the wrong key. To correct this type of error press the **<BACKSPACE>** key which will erase the last character you typed. You may then complete the command. Each time you press <BACKSPACE> a character will be erased. You are typing a DOS command and you see that you have made several errors. Press the **<ESC>** key to cancel the command. Pressing <ESC> cancels the command and allows you to retype the command. You have typed a DOS command and have pressed <ENTER> to begin the operation of the command, but decide that you do not want the command to be completed. You can cancel a DOS command, once it is operating by pressing the key sequence **<CTRL-C>**. You must press and hold down the <CTRL> key, and then press the <C> key. **<CTRL-BREAK>** has the identical function as <CTRL-C> but <CTRL-C> is easier to use.

14 Introduction to DOS

Parameters and Options

The CLS command has no parameters. Most commands have **parameters** that can proceed or follow the command. Parameters usually indicate the target of the command. A target can be a disk-drive name (B:), a file name (COMMAND.COM), or a filespec (B:COMMAND.COM). The file name is the name given to a file on disk. The **file name** consists of a one-to eight-character **filename** and an optional one-to three-character **extension**. If an extension is used, it is connected to the filename with a period (.). A example of a file name is COMMAND.COM. A **filespec** combines a disk-drive name and a file name. An example of a filespec is B:COMMAND.COM. File names will be discussed thoroughly in chapter four. The syntax of a command will show that some parameters are required and some are optional. If a parameter is enclosed in square brackets ([ ]) it is an optional parameter. If the parameter is enclosed in arrow brackets (< >) it is required. If you omit a required parameter, DOS will issue an error message. If you omit an optional parameter, DOS will substitute a default parameter. A **default** is a value that DOS will use if you do not supply a value. Most commands also have **options** (also called switches) which can be used to change the output of a command. Options are always preceded by a slash (/).

DOS Command Syntax

An example of a DOS command is the FORMAT command, which prepares a new disk for use. The partial syntax of the FORMAT command is as follows:

```
Syntax: [D:]FORMAT <D:> [/V]
```

The leading [D:] is an optional drive name indicating which drive contains the command. If this parameter is omitted, DOS will substitute the default drive. FORMAT is the DOS command, the <D:> indicates that a drive name must be specified, and the [/V] is an option of the format command. You do not type either of the brackets when entering a command. If you do not include a drive-name parameter after the FORMAT command, DOS will display an error message. Drive names include A:, B:, and C:. The following command includes a drive parameter directing DOS to format the disk in drive B:

```
FORMAT B:
```

The following command includes the /V option so that DOS will allow you to add an electronic volume label to the disk:

```
FORMAT B:/V
```

If a leading drive name is used in a command, for example, the A:, in the command, A:FORMAT B:/V, the drive name must not have spaces between it and the command. Parameters and options that follow the DOS command must be separated from the command by a delimiter. A **delimiter** is a special character used to define the end of a portion of a DOS command. Delimiters include a space, a slash, a comma, a semicolon, and an equals sign. In the command, A:FORMAT B:/V, the second drive-name parameter is separated by a space, and the volume option is separated by a slash. DOS will display an error if you leave a space after a leading drive name, misspell the DOS command, the drive name, or the option, omit the space after the command, or omit the slash before the option.

Internal and External Commands

When you boot DOS, it loads the DOS system files (MSDOS.SYS, IO.SYS, and COMMAND.COM) into RAM. A set of **internal commands** are part of the COMMAND.COM file which is loaded into RAM. Internal commands are the most commonly used commands and are retrieved from RAM when they are used. An example of an internal command is the CLS command. The **external commands** are a series of DOS programs that are less commonly used than the internal commands. These programs are stored on the boot drive (drive A on a floppy system, or drive C on a hard-disk system). Since these programs are not loaded into RAM, they must be retrieved from the boot drive. An example of an external command is the FORMAT command. If you want to use an external command, you must specify the boot drive as part of the command. For example, the default drive is drive B, and you want to use the FORMAT command to format the disk in drive B. You will have to enter the command as A:FORMAT B: to direct DOS to drive A to find the external command FORMAT.

Booting DOS

Before DOS can be used it must be loaded from disk into RAM. **Booting** loads the system files of DOS into the memory of the computer. Two methods are used to boot DOS. Turning on the power to the microcomputer to boot DOS is called a **cold boot**. If the computer is already turned on but needs to be rebooted, a **warm boot** is used. Both methods of booting use a **bootstrap loader program** stored in ROM to load the DOS system files into RAM. A cold boot takes much longer than a warm boot because the **POST (Power On Start Up) program** stored in ROM is run when the cold boot is done. The POST program checks the RAM chips and keyboard interface for malfunctions. If a malfunction is found, an error message is displayed. A warm boot does not run the POST program.

To cold boot a floppy-disk computer (two floppy disks but no hard disk), the DOS disk is placed in drive A (the upper or left drive if there are two floppy drives) and then the power switch is turned on (on some computers the monitor must also be switched on). The microcomputer then loads the system files of DOS into RAM. On a hard-disk microcomputer, DOS is stored on the hard disk. To cold boot a hard-disk microcomputer (one floppy disk and a hard disk), leave drive door A open when the power is turned on. A cold boot is typically only done once a day because the electronic chips are stressed each time the microcomputer is turned on. Occasionally, your system may lock up and you will have to do a warm boot to restart your system. A warm boot erases RAM and reloads the system files of DOS into RAM. Pressing the <CTRL>, <ALT>, and <DEL> keys simultaneously initiates a warm boot. To warm boot a floppy-disk system, put the DOS diskette in drive A and then press <CTRL-ALT-DEL>. To warm boot a hard-disk microcomputer, press <CTRL-ALT-DEL> with drive door A open. If a warm boot fails to unlock a system, turn the system off, wait twenty seconds, and then attempt to cold boot the microcomputer.

When either a warm boot or a cold boot is used, DOS looks for an optional CONFIG.SYS file on the boot drive (drive A on a floppy-disk system and drive C on a hard-disk system). This file can be used to customize the configuration of your system. For example, many applications programs require a CONFIG.SYS file that changes the default number of files that may be open to a number larger than the DOS default. If the CONFIG.SYS file is found, DOS will execute the commands found in that file. The CONFIG.SYS file is discussed thoroughly in Appendix A. At boot time, DOS also looks on the boot drive for another special file called **AUTOEXEC.BAT**. Advanced users include a series of boot-related commands in the AUTOEXEC.BAT file to simplify the booting process. For example, most microcomputers contain a built-in clock. A command can be included in the AUTOEXEC.BAT file to have DOS read the date and the time from the built-in clock at boot time. If this command is not included in an AUTOEXEC.BAT file, the user will have to type in the date and the time. The AUTOEXEC.BAT file is discussed thoroughly in chapter seven.

16 Introduction to DOS

Date and Time Prompts

If you boot the microcomputer from a hard disk, you will usually not be prompted by DOS to enter the date and the time because DOS will extract the date and the time from the system clock. If you boot the microcomputer from a floppy disk, you will be prompted by DOS to enter the current date and the current time. If you are prompted to enter the date it must be entered in this format: mm-dd-yy. Enter the numeric month (12), numeric day (31), and numeric year (92) separated by dashes and then press <ENTER>. For example, December 31, 1992 would be entered as 12-31-92.   If you are prompted for the time it must be entered in this format: hh:mm. Enter the hour (6) and the minutes (30) separated by a colon and press <ENTER>. For example 6:30 a.m. would be entered as 6:30. DOS uses a 24-hour clock so 6:00 p.m. would be entered as 18:00. For both the date and the time use the numbers on the alphabetic keyboard, not the numbers on the numeric keypad. DOS uses the current date and time to date and time stamp files that are created or modified. If DOS requests the date and you press <ENTER> to skip this step, DOS will date stamp your files with the default date of 01-01-80. You should always enter the correct date and time because, in addition to DOS, many applications programs also use the date and the time.

DOS Prompt

After the date and time have been entered, DOS displays the version number of DOS (for example Version 3.3) and then will display the **DOS prompt**. An example of a DOS prompt is A> on a floppy-disk system and C> on a hard-drive system. The system prompt consists of the disk-drive letter of the boot drive and the greater than symbol (>). The system prompt indicates that DOS has been successfully booted and is ready to receive commands.

Booting Errors

Problem: Nothing displays on the screen when you do a cold boot.
Solution: Make sure that power is turned on to the monitor and/or the brightness/contrast controls on the monitor are set high enough so that the boot screen can be displayed.

Problem: DOS displays the following error message:

```
Non-System or disk error
Replace and strike any key when ready
```

Solution: The disk in drive A is not the DOS disk. Put the DOS disk in drive A and reboot.

Problem: DOS displays one of the following error messages:

```
Invalid date
Enter new date (mm-dd-yy)

or

Invalid time
Enter new time:
```

Solution: You have entered the date or the time incorrectly. Check the tips in the Date and Time Prompt section on page 29 and reenter the date or time.

Changing Drives

The drive that you boot from is called the **default drive**. The DOS prompt displays the current default drive. For example, if the prompt is C>, the default drive is C. When you issue a command, DOS must know which disk drive that command applies to. If you issue a command but do not enter a drive name, DOS will assume the default drive. If you are entering a command that applies to the default drive, you can save keystrokes by omitting the drive name. If you are entering a command that refers to the nondefault drive, you must include the drive name of the nondefault drive in that command. If you booted from drive C, the default drive would be C:. DOS drive names include the letter of the drive followed by a colon (:). Floppy drives are named A: and B: and hard drives are named C: and D:. You can change the default drive by entering a valid drive name followed by a colon (:). The drive that you change to is called the current default drive or **current drive**. For example, this command changes the default drive to drive A:

```
A:
```

Changing Drive Error

Problem: You have entered the command C: to change drives to drive C and DOS displays this error message:

```
INVALID DRIVE SPECIFICATION
```

Solution: Check the drive specification that you typed and make sure that your microcomputer has a drive C.

Commands

DATE Command

```
Syntax: DATE [mm-dd-yy]
```

After the computer has been booted you may notice that the date is incorrect. The **DATE Command**, a DOS internal command, is used to change the date. If you specify a new date when you enter the command, it is changed immediately. If you omit this optional parameter, DOS displays the current date and prompts you to enter a new date. Press <ENTER> if you do not wish to change it. If you enter an invalid date, DOS prompts you to enter a valid date.

TIME Command

```
Syntax: TIME [hh:mm:[:ss]]
```

After the computer has been booted you may notice that the time is incorrect. The **TIME command**, a DOS internal command, is used to change the time. If you specify a new time when you enter the command, it is changed immediately. If you omit the optional parameters, DOS displays the current time and prompts you to enter a new time. Press <ENTER> if you do not wish to change it. If you enter an invalid time, DOS prompts you to enter a valid time. You may enter the hours and minutes and omit the seconds parameter.

18 Introduction to DOS

VER Command

```
Syntax: VER
```

Many applications programs require a particular version of DOS to run correctly. For example, a program may require Version 3 or later of DOS. The **VER (VERsion) command** is a DOS internal command used to display the version of DOS loaded in RAM.

CLS Command

```
Syntax: CLS
```

The **CLS (CLear Screen) command** is an DOS internal command that clears the screen and displays the DOS prompt in the upper left-hand corner of the screen.

PROMPT Command

```
Syntax: PROMPT <Prompt String>
```

Every disk has a single directory, called the **root directory**, created by DOS and used to store the names of the files on that disk. Hard disks are divided up into a series of **subdirectories,** created by the user, which organized the hard disk into different compartments. Each subdirectory is used to store a different group of files. For example, one subdirectory might be used to store word processing files and another would store spreadsheet files. Subdirectories are discussed thoroughly in chapter six. If you are working on a hard-disk system, you need to know in which subdirectory you are currently located. The default DOS prompt (A> on a floppy system and C> on a hard-drive system) displays the default drive followed by a greater than sign. The default prompt tells you the default or current drive but it does not tell you the current directory. The **PROMPT command** is a DOS internal command used to create a custom DOS prompt. This custom prompt can display the current directory and the default drive so that you will always know the current directory by looking at the prompt. The prompt string can consist of text and special strings in the form of $c. The following table summarizes the special strings:

String	Use
p g t d	Displays current directory in a prompt. Displays the > character in a prompt. Displays system time in a prompt. Displays system date in a prompt.

PROMPT strings

The following command would create a custom prompt that displays the current directory followed by the > symbol:

```
PROMPT $P$G
```

The $P part of the prompt string tells DOS to display the current directory (which includes the default drive) and the $G part of the prompt string displays the > character. DOS uses the **backslash symbol** (\) to denote the root directory. For example, if the default drive is drive A and the current directory is the root directory, the prompt displayed would be:

```
A:\>
```

This custom prompt shows that the default drive is A and the current directory is the root directory or A:\. The custom prompt is useful because you will always know the current directory just by looking at the prompt. You will be doing a series of tutorial exercises at the end of each chapter in this text. You may do the tutorials using a floppy-disk computer (two floppy disks and no hard disk) or you may use a hard-disk computer (one floppy disk and a hard disk). If you use a floppy-disk computer to do the exercises, the only directories that you will use will be either the root directory of drive A (A:\) or the root directory of drive B (B:\). If you use a hard disk to do the tutorial exercises, a special subdirectory called \DT will be used for the exercises. This subdirectory has a copy of the DOS external commands. You will enter a command to create a custom prompt as part of each tutorial. If you are using a hard disk for the tutorial you should have the following custom prompt to begin the tutorial:

```
C:\DT>
```

This prompt tells you that you are on drive C and the current directory is C:\DT which is the directory that contains a copy of the DOS external commands. If the current directory is not C:\DT, you must use the following **CD (Change Directory) command** to change the current directory to C:\DT:

```
CD\DT
```

The CD command will be discussed thoroughly in chapter six. If you change from drive C to drive A, the prompt displayed will be A:\>. When you reboot, the default prompt of A> or C> will be displayed. You must enter the PROMPT PG command to restore the custom prompt. The command PROMPT with no parameters will restore the default prompt.

Printing Commands

<SHIFT-PRTSC> {Screen Echo} is a key sequence used to print the current display screen. Press and hold down either of the <SHIFT> keys and then press the <PRTSC> key to print a hard copy of the current screen display. If you are using the original keyboard the <SHIFT-PRTSC> sequence must be used. If you are using the enhanced keyboard the **<PRINT SCREEN>** key will print the current screen display. If you want to print all the information DOS writes to the screen, use the **<CTRL-P>** {Character Echo} key sequence. The <CTRL-P> key sequence is a toggle. If you press <CTRL-P>, you have toggled character echo on. Any characters that you enter are echoed (printed on) to the printer, and any output to the screen from DOS is echoed to the printer. When you initially press <CTRL-P>, nothing happens. The next character you enter is echoed on the printer.

For example, you press <CTRL-P> and then enter the FORMAT command. The FORMAT command and the report generated by the FORMAT command will both be printed. To turn off character echo, press <CTRL-P> again.

Printing Error

Problem: You have entered the command to print the screen or have toggled on character echo with a <CTRL-P> and DOS displays the following error message:

```
Not ready error writing device PRN
Abort, Retry, Ignore, Fail?
```

Solution: Your microcomputer does not have a printer connected to it or the printer is not ready to print. If your microcomputer does not have a printer attached, type A to abort the command. If you have a printer attached, make sure that it is ready to print, and then enter R to retry the command. A printer must be turned on, be switched on-line, and have paper in it before it is ready to print.

Computer Operations Tips

In the tutorial for this chapter you are going to become a microcomputer operator. There are some important things that you should know about the microcomputer hardware and disks to be a successful operator.

Diskettes

A diskette is enclosed in a flexible plastic jacket (5.25 inch) or a hard plastic jacket (3.5 inch). The diskette itself is made of a plastic material that is coated with a magnetic material. Since the diskette is made of plastic, excessive heat will damage it. Since the data on the diskette is recorded magnetically anything that can erase this magnetic field will create problems. When you are not using the 5.25-inch diskette you should place it in its paper diskette cover to protect it from dust, dirt, and prying fingers. The cover also contains lubricants that will increase the life of the diskette. The 3.25-inch diskette is enclosed in a permanent cover.

Follow these rules in handling 5.25-inch diskettes:

1. Many diskettes have a label on them that allows you to identify the diskette. If your diskette does not have a label, prepare one for it. Write on the label before you place it on the diskette. If you write on this label after it has been pasted to the diskette, use a felt-tip pen (other types of pens may harm the diskette). Beware of the layered look. Pasting several labels on top of each other may jam the diskette drive.
2. When handling a diskette, touch only the end that contains the label. Don't ever touch the Head Access area, the oblong hole that is found at the bottom of the diskette. The diskette drive reads and writes through this hole. If you touch this area of the diskette you may have to purchase another diskette. The diskette spins inside its protective cover and the diskette drive accesses the diskette through the Head Access hole.
3. To insert the diskette in the drive follow these steps:
   a. Open the drive door. Full-height drives have a latch located in the middle of the drive door that must be flipped up to open the door. Half-height drives have a handle that must be flipped up to provide access to the diskette drive.
   b. Grasp the diskette by the label end and take it out of its sleeve.
   c. Position the diskette so that the label faces the ceiling. The write-protect notch should be facing left. The end of the diskette facing the drive should have two small semicircular notches.
   d. Gently slide the diskette all the way inside the drive. Do not bend or force the diskette. If you encounter resistance, pull the diskette out and try again. Once the diskette is inside the drive, close the latch on the drive door on a full-height drive or press the handle down on a half-height drive to secure the diskette.
4. To remove the diskette from the drive, follow these steps:
   a. On a full-height drive, flip the latch on the drive door, grasp the diskette with your fingers, and pull it out.
   b. On a half-height drive, turn the handle and a spring will eject the diskette from the drive.
5. When you are not using a diskette, place it in its protective sleeve.
6. Do not bend or place heavy objects on top of the diskette.
7. To protect a diskette from being over-written, place a piece of black or gray tape over the write-protect notch.

22 Introduction to DOS

Follow these rules when handling a 3.5-inch diskette:

```
1. To insert the diskette in the drive, hold it with the arrow
   facing up and forward.  Slide the diskette into the recessed
   opening until it locks in place.
2. To remove the diskette from the drive press the button found
   under the recessed opening and the diskette will be ejected.
3. To protect a diskette from being over-written, turn the
   diskette over so that the manufacturer's label faces down
   and forward.  Press down on the tab found on the lower right-
   hand side of the diskette.
```

Follow these rules when handling either type of diskette:

```
1. Diskettes should be stored vertically in a box or some other
   protective container.
2. Keep diskettes away from:
   a. Magnetic fields such as television sets, telephones, tele-
      phone answering machines, and fans.  Most appliances will
      not affect your diskettes, unless you store your diskettes
      near them for a long time.  Keep your diskettes at least
      one foot away from magnetic fields, increasing the dis-
      tance away from more powerful appliances.
   b. Direct sunlight or excessive heat or cold.  If your
      diskettes are exposed to temperatures of less than fifty
      degrees F., let them warm up before using them.  Cold
      diskettes become rigid and shrink slightly.  This is a
      problem particularly with the high-density 5.25-inch
      diskettes.
   c. Don't eat or drink near the microcomputer.  A coffee or
      soft drink spill could ruin your diskette or damage the
      microcomputer.
```

Diskette Drives

```
1. When the in-use light is on, do not insert or remove disk-
   ettes.  The light indicates that the drive is attempting to
   read from or write to a diskette.  If you interrupt the disk-
   ette drive when the light is on you may ruin the diskette,
   the drive, or both.
2. On 5.25-inch drives, if there is not a diskette in the
   drive, do not close the drive door or flip the latch to the
   closed position.
```

Hard Disk Drives

> 1. Hard-disk drives are quite delicate. Do not jar a computer that contains a hard-disk drive.
> 2. The hard-disk drive should be parked before you turn off the computer.

Monitors

> 1. Do not touch the screen with your fingers or any objects.
> 2. Use the contrast controls to adjust the picture.
> 3. If you leave the computer, turn the screen off.

Dot Matrix Printers

> 1. Do not use the platen handle found on the side of the printer to advance the paper. If the printer is on, using this wheel may damage the printer.
> 2. Keep your fingers away from the print head.
> 3. Do not try to change paper or adjust ribbons yourself.
> 4. The printer must be turned on for it to work. There are usually several lights that are found on the top or front of the printer. If all these lights are off, the printer is probably not turned on.
> 5. The printer must also be on-line to print information. The printer may be turned on but may not be on-line. The lights on the printer control panel will indicate if the printer is on-line or off-line.
> 6. There are two control buttons that are used to advance the paper. The line-feed button advances the paper one line. The form-feed button advances the paper one whole sheet.
> 7. To ensure that your printout starts at the top of the sheet, you must have the printer at top of form.

Laser Printers

> 1. Do not open up the laser printer because it is hot inside.
> 2. The printer must be on and on-line to print information. If the printer is on-line the On Line button will be lit.
> 3. To advance paper out of the printer, press the On Line button and then press the Form Feed button. After you have removed your printout, press the On Line button again.

Terms

AUTOEXEC.BAT (15)
Backslash symbol (\) (19)
Booting (15)
Bootstrap loader program (15)
CD (Change Directory) command (19)
CLS (Clear Screen) command (18)
Cold boot (15)
COMMAND.COM (13)
CONFIG.SYS (13)
Current drive (17)
DATE command (17)
Default (14)
Default drive (17)
Delimiter (14)
DOS command (13)
DOS command processor (13)
DOS prompt (16)
DOS system files (13)
Extension (14)
External commands (15)
File name (14)
Filename (14)
Filespec (14)
Hidden files (13)
Internal commands (15)
IO.SYS (13)
MSDOS.SYS (13)
Options (14)
Parameters (14)
POST (Power On Start Up) program (15)
PROMPT command (18)
Root directory (18)
Subdirectories (18)
TIME command (17)
VER (VERsion) command (18)
Warm boot (15)
<BACKSPACE> (13)
<CTRL-BREAK> (13)
<CTRL-C> (13)
<CTRL-P> (19)
<ESC> (13)
<PRINT SCREEN> (19)
<SHIFT-PRTSC> (19)

Review Questions

Name _____

Mastery Self-Quiz True/False

Answer T for true or F for false.

1. **T** COMMAND.COM is a DOS system file.
2. **F** DOS commands must be typed in uppercase.
3. **T** Pressing <BACKSPACE> will erase the last character you typed.
4. **T** The default DOS prompt displays the name of the default drive.
5. **T** Booting loads the system files of DOS into RAM.
6. **F** Pressing <CTRL-ALT-DEL> does a cold boot.
7. **T** The CLS command has no parameters.
8. **F** CLS clears the screen and RAM.
9. **T** If you have not pressed <ENTER>, the <ESC> key can be used to cancel a DOS command.
10. **T** If you have pressed <ENTER>, pressing <CTRL-C> will cancel the current DOS command.
    CTRL-B

Mastery Self-Quiz Fill-in

1. The drive that you boot from is known as the ___default___ drive.
2. Command options must be preceded by the _____ character.
3. A ___default___ is a value that DOS will use if you do not supply a value.
4. A ___delimiter___ is a special character used to define the end of a portion of a DOS command.
5. The command ___PG___ will create a custom prompt that displays the current directory.
6. The root directory is denoted by this symbol _____.
7. The ___a:___ command changes the default drive to drive A.
8. The ___c:___ command changes the default drive to drive C.
9. The ___ver___ command displays the version of DOS.
10. The ___Date___ command is used to change the system date.

Discussion Questions

1. Explain the difference between internal and external commands.

   internal — command.com

   external — disk

2. Explain the difference between a cold boot and a warm boot.

   — post

   — Ram

3. Identify the keys or key sequences that can be used to correct or cancel DOS commands.

26 Introduction to DOS

Solving Error Messages

Enter the solution to each of these problems.

Problem: Nothing displays on the screen when you do a cold boot.

Solution:

Problem: DOS displays the following error message:

```
Non-System or disk error
Replace and strike any key when ready
```

Solution:

Problem: DOS displays one of the following error messages:

```
Invalid date
Enter new date (mm-dd-yy)

or

Invalid time
Enter new time:
```

Solution:

Problem: You have entered the command C: to change drives to drive C and DOS displays this error message:

```
INVALID DRIVE SPECIFICATION
```

Solution:

Problem: You have entered the command to print the screen or have toggled on character echo with a <CTRL-P> and DOS displays the following message:

```
Not ready error writing device PRN
Abort, Retry, Ignore, Fail?
```

Solution:

Chapter Two Tutorial

Tutorial Explanation

You are now going to do the first of the tutorial lessons. These lessons will be done using the computer. To follow the tutorial steps accurately you should be aware of the following:

1. Enter each step in the sequence shown.
2. Whenever a key is used in the tutorial it will be shown bracketed by the < character and the > character. The key name will always be capitalized. For example, the ESC key will be shown as <ESC>.
3. The information that you must enter is printed in **boldface**. You will key in exactly what is shown in **boldface**. An example would be: Press: **<ESC>**. This step indicates that you must press the **<ESC>** key. All the information that you must enter is shown in UPPERCASE. You may use lowercase or uppercase or a mixture of uppercase or lowercase.
4. Often you must complete the entry of information by pressing the <ENTER> key or an arrow key. The tutorial will always show that <ENTER> must be pressed by this notation: <ENTER>. For example the following is a tutorial step:

    ENTER: **CLS   <ENTER>**

    This notation means type CLS and then press <ENTER>.

5. When two keys bracketed together are separated by a hyphen, press and hold down the first key and then press the second key. For example, the tutorial shows the following:

    PRESS: **<SHIFT-PRTSC>**

    Press and hold down <SHIFT> and then press <PRTSC>.

6. After you have completed some steps you will be asked to match your screen with a screen displayed in the tutorial. If your screen does not match, check with your instructor or computer center personnel. The following is an example of a screen display:

```
Current date is SUN 12-31-91
Enter new date (mm-dd-yy):
```

Hardware

There are two types of computer systems:

```
1. A floppy-disk system with an A drive and a B drive.
2. A hard-disk system with a hard disk an A drive.
```

There are two types of floppy-disk drives:

```
1. 5.25-inch drives.
2. 3.5-inch drives.
```

You must ask your instructor or computer center personnel which type of system (hard disk or floppy disk), and which type of disk drive (5.25 or 3.5), you will use for the tutorial. Also find out if you must turn on the monitor. Use this information to fill out the following chart:

```
Enter system type (hard or floppy) _____
Enter the type of disk drive of drive A (5.25 or 3.5) _____
Does the monitor have to be switched on (yes or no) _____
```

If you are using a floppy-disk system, you will follow the steps labeled floppy-disk users. If you are using a hard-disk system, you will follow the steps labeled hard-disk users. If you are using a hard-disk system turn to page 33, otherwise do the instructions that follow.

Floppy-Disk Users

If the disk drives are not clearly marked drive A and drive B, you must ask your instructor or computer center personnel to identify drive A and drive B. Drive A is usually the upper or left-most drive. Check out a DOS system disk that matches your drive type (5.25 or 3.5).

Inserting Disks

If you are using a 3.5-inch disk, go to the section marked "inserting a 3.5-inch disk", otherwise do the following:

1. Locate the DOS system disk and take the disk out of its paper envelope. Be sure to handle the disk by the label end only. Hold the disk by the label end with the label facing the ceiling.
2. Put the DOS system disk in drive A and secure the disk. Securing the disk means that you either close a drive door or flip a lever down.
3. Go to the Cold Boot section.

Inserting a 3.5-inch disk

1. Locate the DOS system disk. The 3.5-inch disks have an arrow on the upper left-hand side of the disk. Hold the disk with the arrow facing up and forward and slide the disk into the disk drive.

Cold Boot

Once a day you will have to turn on the systems unit. When you turn on the systems unit with the DOS system disk in drive A, the microcomputer performs a cold boot. When you cold boot a microcomputer, the ROM POST program is run. This program checks the hardware devices attached to your system and displays error messages if they are not working properly. If all the hardware is in order, the DOS system files are loaded into RAM. The following steps are used to cold boot a floppy-disk system.

1. If necessary, turn on the monitor (display screen).
2. If the microcomputer is off, turn it on. If the microcomputer is turned on, turn it off, count to twenty and turn it on again. You may wait up to two minutes before anything occurs. If the system is successfully booted it will display a date prompt.

Date and Time Prompts

1. DOS should display the following date prompt (your date will not match the date shown):

```
Current date is SUN 12-31-91
Enter new date (mm-dd-yy):
```

2. Type in the current date using the following tips:
   a. If the current date was December 12, 1991, you would type 12-31-91.
   b. Do not type leading zeros.
   c. Use a hyphen between the numbers.
   d. Use the number keys located on the top row of the keyboard.
   e. Do not use the letter "O" for zero or the letter "L" for one.
   f. Do not leave spaces in the date.
   g. Do not enter the day of the week (SUN).
3. PRESS: <ENTER>
   [Enters the date. If you entered the date correctly, DOS will display a time prompt and you can go to step four. If you entered the date incorrectly DOS will display the error message: INVALID DATE. Go back to step two and follow the tips to enter the date correctly.]
4. DOS displays the following prompt:

```
Current time is 16:05:39
Enter new time:
```

5. Type in the current time using the following tips:
   a. DOS uses a twenty-four-hour clock; hence you will not enter a.m. or p.m.
   b. If the time is 6:00 a.m., you will enter 6:00. If the time is 6:00 p.m., you will enter 18:00.
   c. Use a colon between the hours and the seconds.
   d. Use the <SHIFT> key to select the colon.
6. PRESS: <ENTER>
   [Enters the time. If you entered the time incorrectly DOS will display the error message: INVALID TIME. Follow the tips in step five to enter the time correctly.]
7. If you enter the time correctly DOS will display the version of DOS being used and the following DOS prompt:

30 Introduction to DOS

```
A>
```

Warm Boot

A warm boot is used if the computer locks up and you cannot unlock it. A warm boot erases RAM and reloads the DOS system files into RAM. The following steps are used to warm boot a microcomputer.

1. PRESS: **<CTRL-ALT>**
   [Press the <CTRL> key and the <ALT> key and hold them down. The <CTRL> and <ALT> keys are found on the bottom left portion of the keyboard.]
2. PRESS: **<DEL>**
   [While holding down <CTRL> and <ALT>, tap the <DEL> key. The <DEL> key is found on the far right side of the keyboard. This key sequence is known as the <CTRL-ALT-DEL> warm-boot sequence.]
3. DOS displays the following:

```
Current Date is SUN 12-31-91
Enter New Date (mm-dd-yy):
```

4. Type the current date and press <ENTER>.
5. DOS displays the following:

```
Current time is 16:05:39
Enter new time:
```

6. Type the current time and press <ENTER>.
7. DOS displays the current version of DOS being used and displays the following DOS prompt:

```
A>
```

Clear the Screen

The CLS command clears the display screen and displays the DOS prompt in the upper left-hand corner of the display screen. Remember that the notation <ENTER> means press the <ENTER> key.

1. TYPE: **CLS** <ENTER>
   [The screen clears and the DOS prompt is redisplayed.]

Custom Prompt

DOS displays a default prompt of A> which indicates the default drive (the A portion of the prompt) and that you are in DOS (the > portion of the prompt). A hard disk is divided into several directories and if you are using a hard disk it is very important to know which directory you are currently using. A floppy disk typically has only one directory called the root directory. DOS denotes the root directory with the backslash symbol (\). You are going to enter a command to change the DOS prompt so that it also displays the current directory. This information will not be of much use to you until you reach chapter six when you will create floppy-disk directories. If you do use a hard-disk system, you will find this custom prompt quite useful. When you type the PROMPT command, remember to leave a space between the PROMPT command and the parameters of PG.

1. TYPE: **PROMPT PG** <ENTER>
    [DOS should display the following custom prompt (the \ indicates that the current directory is the root directory:]

```
A:\>
```

Changing the Date and Time

The DATE and TIME commands are used to check the current date and time and if necessary, change them.

1. TYPE: **DATE** <ENTER>
    [DOS will display the date prompt.]
2. PRESS: **<ENTER>**
    [You could have changed the date at this point.]
3. TYPE: **TIME** <ENTER>
    [DOS will display the time prompt (note that DOS is continually updating the time).]
4. PRESS: **<ENTER>**
    [You could have changed the time at this point.]
5. TYPE: **CLS** <ENTER>

Displaying the Version of DOS

Some programs require a particular version of DOS. The VER command is used to display the version of DOS loaded in RAM.

1. TYPE: **VER** <ENTER>
    [Your version may differ but DOS will display a line like the following:]

```
MS-DOS Version 3.30
```

32 Introduction to DOS

Correcting and Canceling Commands

The <BACKSPACE> key can be used to erase the character to the left of the cursor in a DOS command so that you may correct the command. The <ESC> key can be used to cancel a DOS command so that you may type another command. Be careful not to press <ENTER> in this section until you are told to do so.

1.   TYPE: **CLSD**
2.   PRESS: **<BACKSPACE>**
   [Pressing <BACKSPACE> erased the character to the left of the cursor in your DOS command. The command typed should now read CLS.]
3.   PRESS: **<ENTER>**
   [You executed the CLS command. The screen should be cleared.]
4.   TYPE: **VER**
5.   PRESS: **<ESC>**
   [Pressing <ESC> cancels the DOS command that you typed. DOS displays a backslash (\) and advances to the next line on the screen.]
6.   TYPE: **CLS <ENTER>**
7.   You have now completed the tutorial. You can either go back to the beginning of the section called floppy disk users on page 28 and do it again, or do comprehensive problem two on page 36.

Hard-Disk Users

Check Drive A and make sure that it is empty (make sure that no diskette is loaded into the drive). If you are using a 5.25-inch drive make sure that it is unlatched or open. Turn the monitor on if necessary.

Cold Boot

Once a day you will have to turn on the systems unit. When you turn on the systems unit without a disk in drive A, the microcomputer performs a cold boot. When you cold boot a microcomputer, the ROM POST program is run. This program checks the hardware devices attached to your system and displays error messages if they are not working properly. If all the hardware is in order, the DOS system files are loaded in to RAM. The following steps are used to cold boot a microcomputer:

1. If necessary, turn on the monitor (display screen).
2. If the microcomputer is off, turn it on. If the microcomputer is turned on, turn it off, count to twenty and turn it on again. You may wait up to two minutes before anything occurs. If the system is successfully booted it will either display a menu or it will display the version of DOS being used and a DOS prompt similar to the following:

Warm Boot

A warm boot is used if the computer locks up and you cannot unlock it. A warm boot erases RAM and reloads the DOS system files into RAM. The following steps are used to warm boot a microcomputer.

1. Press: **<CTRL-ALT>**
   [Press the <CTRL> key and the <ALT> key and hold them down. The <CTRL> and <ALT> keys are found on the bottom left portion of the keyboard.]
2. Press: **<DEL>**
   [While holding down <CTRL> and <ALT>, tap the <DEL> key. The <DEL> key is found on the far right side of the keyboard. This key sequence is known as the <CTRL-ALT-DEL> warm boot sequence.]
3. If the system displays the DOS system prompt of C> go to the section marked Change to C:\DT. If the system displays a menu, check with your instructor or computer center personnel to find out how you can exit the menu to DOS.

Custom Prompt

DOS defaults to a prompt of C> which indicates that you are in DOS and the default drive is drive C. When you are using a hard-disk computer it is very important that you know which directory on the hard disk you are in. You are only going to use one directory on the hard disk, a directory called C:\DT. The following steps will be used to display a custom prompt so that you can determine the current directory by looking at the prompt. When you type in the PROMPT command, be sure to leave a space between the command PROMPT and the parameters of PG. Remember that the notation <ENTER> means that you must press the <ENTER> key.

1. TYPE: **PROMPT PG** <ENTER>
2. DOS will display a custom prompt that displays the default drive and the default directory. Your prompt should be similar to the following prompt:

34 Introduction to DOS

```
C:\DT>
```

3. If your prompt matches the C:\DT> prompt exactly you can skip to the section called Clear the Screen. If your prompt does not match C:\DT> you must do the next section called Change to C:\DT.

Change to C:\DT

A hard disk is divided up into several different directories. As a beginning DOS student, you will only work in one directory called C:\DT. You must do the following steps to change to the C:\DT directory.

1. TYPE: **CD\DT** <ENTER>
2. DOS should display the following prompt:

```
C:\DT>
```

3. If your prompt does not match the C:\DT> prompt, check with your instructor or computer center personnel and do not do any more steps until you have the C:\DT> prompt.

Clear the Screen

The CLS command clears the display screen and displays the DOS prompt in the upper left-hand corner of the display screen. Remember that the notation <ENTER> means press the <ENTER> key.

1. TYPE: **CLS** <ENTER>
    [The screen clears and the DOS prompt is redisplayed.]

Changing the Date and Time

The DATE and TIME commands are used to check the current date and time and, if necessary, change them.

1. TYPE: **DATE** <ENTER>
2. DOS should display the following date prompt (your date will not match the date shown):

```
Current date is SUN 12-31-91
Enter new date (mm-dd-yy):
```

3. Type in the current date using the following tips:
   a. If the current date was December 12, 1991, you would type 12-31-91.
   b. Do not type leading zeros.
   c. Use a hyphen between the numbers.
   d. Use the number keys located on the top row of the keyboard.
   e. Do not use the letter "O" for zero or the letter "L" for one.
   f. Do leave spaces in the date.
   g. Do not enter the day of the week (SUN).
4. PRESS: **<ENTER>**
   [Enters the date. If you entered the date correctly, DOS will display a time prompt and you can go to step five. If you entered the date incorrectly DOS will display the error message: INVALID DATE. Go back to step three and follow the tips to enter the date correctly.]
5. TYPE: **TIME** <ENTER>
6. DOS displays the following prompt (your time will not match the time shown):

```
Current time is 16:05:39
Enter new time:
```

7. Type in the current time using the following tips:
   a. DOS uses a twenty-four-hour clock; hence you will not enter a.m. or p.m.
   b. If the time is 6:00 a.m., you will enter 6:00. If the time is 6:00 p.m., you will enter 18:00.
   c. You must use a colon between the hours and the seconds.
   d. Use the <SHIFT> key to select the colon.
8. PRESS: **<ENTER>**
   [Enters the time. If you entered the time incorrectly DOS will display the error message: INVALID TIME. Follow the tips in step six to enter the time correctly.]
9. TYPE: **CLS** <ENTER>
   [DOS should display the prompt C:\DT>.]

Displaying the Version of DOS

Some programs require a particular version of DOS. The VER command is used to display the version of DOS loaded in RAM.

1. TYPE: **VER** <ENTER>
   [Your version may differ but DOS will display a line like the following:]

```
MS-DOS Version 3.30
```

Correcting and Canceling Commands

The <BACKSPACE> key can be used to erase the character to the left of the cursor in a DOS command so that you may correct the command. The <ESC> key can be used to cancel a DOS command so that you may type another command. Be careful not to press <ENTER> in this section until you are told to do so.

1. TYPE: **CLSD**
2. PRESS: **<BACKSPACE>**
   [Pressing <BACKSPACE> erased the character to the left of the cursor in your DOS command. The command typed should now read CLS.]

36 Introduction to DOS

3.   PRESS: <ENTER>
   [You executed the CLS command. The screen should be cleared.]
4.   TYPE: VER
5.   PRESS: <ESC>
   [Pressing <ESC> cancels the DOS command that you typed. DOS displays a backslash (\) and advances to the next line on the screen.]
6.   TYPE: CLS <ENTER>
7.   You have now completed the tutorial. You can go back to the beginning of the hard-disk users section on page 33 and do the tutorial again, or do comprehensive problem two in the next section.

Comprehensive Problem Two

1. You must be connected to a printer to do this problem.
2. Clear the screen.
3. Use the DATE command to check the date and then press <ENTER>.
4. Use the TIME command to check the time and then press <ENTER>.
5. Use the VER to display the version of DOS.
6. Use the PROMPT command to create a custom prompt that displays the current directory, the > symbol, the date, and the time.
7. Print the screen. Your screen should match the following (floppy-disk users should match the first screen and hard-disk users should match the second screen). The time and the version may not match exactly.

```
A:\>date
Current date is Tue  3-26-1991
Enter new date (mm-dd-yy):

A:\>time
Current time is  9:54:40.80
Enter new time:

A:\>ver

MS-DOS Version 3.30

A:\>prompt $p$g$d $t

A:\>Thu  12-31-92  0:01:10.74
```

Floppy-disk users screen.

```
C:\DT>date
Current date is Tue  3-26-1991
Enter new date (mm-dd-yy):

C:\DT>time
Current time is  9:54:40.80
Enter new time:

C:\DT>ver

MS-DOS Version 3.30

C:\DT>prompt $p$g$d $t

C:\DT>Thu   12-31-92   0:01:10.74
```

Hard-disk users screen.

1. You have completed the tutorial. Follow the system shut-down steps.

System Shut-Down

```
1. Make sure that the in-use light is off for all disk drives.
2. If there is a diskette in drive A, open the drive door A and
   remove the diskette.
3. If there is a diskette in drive B, open the drive door B and
   remove the diskette.
4. If you have a monitor with an on/off switch, switch the
   monitor off. If you have a monitor without an on/off switch,
   turn the contrast control to the left until the display just
   about disappears.
5. Do not turn the computer off.
6. Return any diskettes that you have checked out.
```

Formatting Disks

Chapter 3

Learning Objectives

After completing chapter three you will be able to:

```
1. Define track, sector, and cluster.
2. Define directory and File Allocation Table (FAT).
3. Use FORMAT to prepare a new disk for use.
4. Use the FORMAT/V option to put a volume label on a disk.
5. Use the FORMAT/S option to create a system disk.
6. Use FORMAT options to format double-density disks in high-
   density drives.
7. Use VOL to check the volume label.
8. Use LABEL to add, change, or delete a volume label.
9. Use PATH to set an extended search path for DOS.
```

FORMAT Command

```
Syntax: [D:]FORMAT <D:> [/V] [/S] [/4] [/T:xx] [/N:x]
```

The **FORMAT command** is a DOS external command used to prepare a new disk for use. A new disk (floppy or hard) cannot be used until it is formatted. Because the FORMAT command erases any existing data on a disk, use extreme caution when using this command. FORMAT is typically used to format diskettes in either drive A or drive B. Please do not use the FORMAT command to format drive C unless you have been instructed to do so. FORMAT creates areas on the disk that are used to store data called **tracks** and **sectors**. Tracks are invisible concentric rings and the tracks are segmented into pie-shaped sectors. Tracks and sectors are written on both the bottom of the disk (side 0) and the top of the disk (side 1). The number of tracks and sectors created by FORMAT is determined by the version of DOS used, the type of disk drive used to format the disk, and the options specified with the FORMAT command. A 5.25-inch double-density disk is formatted with forty tracks and each track is divided into nine sectors. FORMAT determines if there are any **bad sectors** on the disk and marks them as not usable. FORMAT creates two areas on the disk called the **directory** (also called the root directory) and the **File Allocation Table (FAT)** that are used to keep track of the data that is stored and keep track of the location of the bad sectors. The directory stores information about files written on the disk. The directory is a table of contents of the disk. The FAT stores the location of bad sectors. The FAT is an index as to the usable areas of the disk. The FORMAT command performs the following steps when it formats a disk (a double-density 5.25-inch floppy disk is used as an example):

> 1. Invisible concentric rings called tracks are laid down on the disk surface and are divided into pie-shaped sectors. Forty tracks are created on both sides of the disk. Each track is divided into nine sectors for a total of 360 sectors on each side. Each sector can store 512 bytes of data.
> 2. FORMAT writes on each sector of the disk to determine if it is usable. Bad sectors are marked as unusable.
> 3. The directory area (called the root directory) is created. The directory will store information about files stored on the disk. The information stored on each file includes the file name, the file size in bytes, the date and time the file was created or last modified, and the location of the beginning of the file data on the disk.
> 4. The File Allocation Table (FAT) is created. The FAT stores the location of bad sectors, identifies which sectors belong to which files, and which sectors can be used to store new data.
> 5. FORMAT creates a boot record on the first sector of the disk (side 0, track 0, sector 1). The boot record stores information about the format structure of the disk and contains the bootstrap program.

Once the disk is formatted, five types of sectors exist on the disk: **boot record sector**, directory sector, FAT sectors, bad sectors, and **data sectors** (where file data will be stored). The boot record sector, directory sector, and FAT sectors are called disk overhead because they reduce the amount of data that can be stored on a disk.

Tracks, Sectors, and Clusters

Once a disk has been formatted it can be used to store files. Files that the user creates using application programs are called **data files** because they contain data. The files that contain DOS programs or applications programs are called **program files** because the files contain commands rather than data. The user must store on disk and retrieve from disk data files while using any application program. DOS has file management commands that store files on disk and retrieve them from disk. DOS writes data on both sides of disk. DOS divides a disk into tracks and sectors but it stores data one **cluster** at a time. A cluster (also called a **cylinder**) is the smallest addressable location that can be used to store data on disk. Two sectors (one on each side of the disk) are combined to make up a cluster. Since a 360KB diskette has sector size of 512 bytes, the size of a cluster is 1,024 bytes. Read/write heads are used by the disk drive to read and write to disk. By recording on both sides of the diskette before moving to another track, recording head movement is minimized, and the recording speed is increased. The sector size remains constant no matter which type of disk is used (floppy or hard). The size of a cluster may vary depending upon the type of disk drive used and the number of read/write heads per track. Hard disks typically use cluster sizes of four sectors or 2,048 bytes per cluster. Larger cluster sizes increase the speed of disk access but may waste space when a file is smaller than a cluster.

When you tell DOS to save a file, DOS reads the directory section of the disk to determine an appropriate location to save the file. If the file is a new file, DOS writes the name of the file into the directory and then tries to locate enough unused clusters to store the file. If the file was previously saved to the same disk, DOS writes over the previous file with the updated file that is in RAM. Because DOS may not have enough unused contiguous or consecutive clusters to store the entire file, it may store the file in clusters that are noncontiguous. Files stored in noncontiguous clusters are called **fragmented files** because they are stored in several fragments. The speed of disk access will be slowed down considerably as the number of fragmented files increases because additional head movement will be required to access these files. In chapter five, a technique that can be used to unfragment a floppy disk will be discussed. Each file's entry in the disk directory points to another special section of the disk, called the File Allocation Table (FAT). The FAT entry stores the physical location of the file. To retrieve a file from disk, the user gives DOS the filename and it will search the directory. If DOS finds the filename, it searches the FAT for the physical location of the file and then reads the file into RAM. If DOS does not find the filename, the following error message is displayed:

```
File Not Found
```

Enhancing DOS

DOS has no ability to unfragment a hard disk. Several third-party software packages (for example, PC-TOOLS) have programs that will unfragment a hard disk. A hard-disk system may be slowed down by thirty percent if the hard disk is highly fragmented.

FORMAT Options

The following table summarizes the FORMAT options:

Option	Use
/V /S /4 /T:80/N:9	Formats the disk with a volume label. Formats the disk as a system disk. Formats a double-density 5.25-inch disk in a high-density 5.25-inch drive. Formats a double-density 3.5-inch disk in a high-density 3.5-inch drive

Format a Data Diskette

If you use the FORMAT command without the /S option, DOS will format a **data diskette** that has its entire surface reserved for data. The following command will format a data diskette in drive B:

```
FORMAT B:
```

When the FORMAT command has completed its work, it displays a report showing the total amount of usable bytes on the disk and the amount of bad sectors (if any). After the disk is formatted (assuming a double-density 5.25-inch disk) the following report will be displayed by FORMAT.

```
Format complete

362496 bytes total disk space
362496 bytes available on disk

Format another (Y/N)?
```

This report shows that the disk has 362,496 bytes are available for use. If you wish to format another diskette type Y and press <ENTER>, otherwise type N and press <ENTER>. You should format several diskettes because a diskette can become full when you are trying to save a file and will not accept any more data. If you have another formatted diskette, you can use that diskette to store the file.

FORMAT /V Option

If you use the **FORMAT /V option** to format a disk, you will be able to enter an internal electronic volume label on the diskette. You can display the label on the screen with the **VOL command** without having to remove the diskette from the drive, a requirement with the external label pasted on the diskette. The following command formats a data disk in drive B with a volume label:

```
FORMAT B:/V
```

FORMAT /S Option

In a few cases you will format a diskette with the **FORMAT /S option** so that the DOS system files will be copied to the disk, making it a bootable disk. This type of diskette is called a **system diskette**. A system diskette would be necessary if you wanted to load an application program and DOS onto the same diskette and boot from that diskette. With both DOS and the application program on one diskette you can boot DOS without using a separate DOS diskette. The following command will format a system diskette in drive B:

```
FORMAT B:/S
```

The /S option should not be used if you are formatting a data disk because the DOS system files will occupy storage space on the disk. For example, Version 3.3 system files occupy 78,848 bytes on a diskette. Two options can be used in the same command. The order of the options is not important, either /V/S or /S/V could be used. The following command will format a system diskette with a volume label on drive B:

```
FORMAT B:/V/S
```

FORMAT /4, /T:, and /N: Options

When the FORMAT command is used without the [/4], [/T:], or [/N:] options the type of diskette drive determines the amount of data that can be stored on the disk. A 360KB drive formats a 360KB diskette, a 1.2MB drive formats a 1.2MB disk and so forth. When you format a disk, it should be formatted on your own microcomputer or on one that has the same type of disk drive as yours. For example, if your computer has a 5.25-inch high-density drive, you should format a disk for use in that drive by using your microcomputer or some other microcomputer that has a 5.25-inch high-density drive. You should also use the appropriate type of disk (high-density diskettes in high-density drives). Diskettes formatted in double-density drives (360KB or 720KB) can be read by high-density drives. Double-density diskettes cannot be formatted in high-density drives (1.2MB or 1.44MB) unless you use special options as part of the FORMAT command. If you must format a 5.25-inch double-density disk in a 5.25-high-density drive, use the following FORMAT command with the **FORMAT /4 option** (assuming that the high-density drive is drive A):

```
FORMAT A:/4
```

This command formats the disk with forty tracks on each side rather than the eighty tracks that a high-density drive defaults to. A 5.25-inch double-density disk formatted in a high-density drive can be reliably read by other 5.25-inch high-density drives but cannot be reliably read by 5.25-inch double-density drives. If you have access to a double-density drive, use this drive to format double-density diskettes. If you have a high-density 3.5-inch disk drive and you must format a double-density 3.5-inch disk the following FORMAT command using the **FORMAT /T:80/N:9 option** must be used (assuming that the high-density drive is drive A):

```
FORMAT A:/T:80/N:9
```

This command formats the double-density disk as a 720KB disk rather than a normal high-density 1.44MB disk. This disk can be reliably read by both 720KB drives and 1.44MB drives. The /T:80 and /N:9 options are only available in Version 3.3 or later of DOS.

Write-Protect Status

Diskettes can be **write-protected** so that a drive can read the diskette but cannot erase or write information on the diskette. If you want to write-protect a 5.25-inch diskette, place a write-protect tab (provided with the diskette when it is purchased) over the **write-protect notch**. You can unwrite-protect the diskette by removing the write-protect tab. To write-protect a 3.5-inch diskette you must push the plastic write-protect slide down to open the **write-protect window**. If the write-protect window is open, the diskette drive will refuse to write on the diskette. To unwrite-protect the diskette push the write-protect slide up to close the window.

Formatting Errors

Problem: When the FORMAT command attempts to format a disk, it displays this error message:

```
Attempted write-protect violation
Format Failure
Format another (Y/N)?
```

Solution: Check to see if the diskette is correctly inserted in the drive, the disk latch is closed, and then see if the diskette is write-protected. If the diskette is write-protected but you determine that it can be used, change the write-protect status (remove the write-protect tab on a 5.25-inch diskette or close the write-protect window on a 3.5-inch diskette) and attempt to format it again.

Problem: After the format is complete, DOS displays the following screen:

```
Format Complete

362496 bytes total disk space
  5120 bytes in bad sectors
357376 bytes available on disk
```

Solution: Format the disk again. If DOS still reports bad sectors, the disk is not reliable. If it is a new disk, return it for a refund. If it is not a new disk, discard the disk, because it is not reliable.

Problem: FORMAT displays this error message when it attempts to format a diskette:

```
Invalid media or Track 0 bad - disk unusable
Format Failure
Format another
```

Solution: This can be caused by attempting to format high-density diskettes in double-density drives. If you are attempting to format a double-density diskette in a high-density drive, you must use the [/4], or the [/T:80] and [/N:9] options. If these options fail to solve the problem, you have a bad diskette that must be discarded.

Formatting a Hard Disk

The FORMAT command is one of the commands initially used to prepare a hard disk for use. Consult the DOS manual for the procedures used to format a hard disk. Once the hard drive has been formatted do not use the FORMAT command on a hard disk because it will erase the hard disk. Always use the FORMAT command with a drive parameter. Using Version 3.1 of DOS or earlier versions if the default drive is drive C and you issue this command, DOS will assume that you want to format drive C.

```
FORMAT
```

Versions 3.2 and later of DOS no longer assume that you want to format the default drive. If you enter the FORMAT command without a drive parameter, these versions of DOS refuse to format the disk and will display the following error message:

```
Drive letter must be specified
```

VOL Command

```
Syntax: VOL [D:]
```

The **VOL (VOLume) command** is an internal DOS command used to display the volume label on a disk so that you don't have to physically remove the disk from the drive to identify it. If you do not specify a drive, the default drive is assumed. The following command will display the volume label of the disk in drive B:

```
VOL B:
```

LABEL Command

```
Syntax: [D:]LABEL [D:] [Volume Label]
```

The **LABEL command** is an external DOS command used to add, change, or delete a volume label without reformatting the disk. The LABEL command is only available in Version 3 or later of DOS. If you do not specify the optional label parameter, DOS displays the current label, if any. It then prompts you to enter a label or to press <ENTER> to delete the existing label. The following command will allow the user to add, change, or delete a volume label on a disk in drive B:

```
LABEL B:
```

Path Command

```
Syntax: PATH [D:][path][;path][;path]
```

When a disk is formatted DOS creates a main directory called the root directory. If you have a floppy disk system your disks will typically just have a root directory. The root directory will be A:\ on disks in drive A and B:\ on disks in drive B. If you have a hard-disk system, you must create user directories called subdirectories. The creation and use of subdirectories will be discussed in chapter six. When you boot DOS, the default search path is set to the current directory of the default disk. This means that DOS will only search the current directory of the default disk for an external DOS command. The **PATH command** is a DOS internal command used to extend the search path that DOS uses to find DOS external commands. The DOS external commands will be on the root directory of drive A (A:\) on a floppy disk system, or in a subdirectory (usually C:\DOS) on a hard-disk system. You are using a floppy-disk system with the DOS system disk in drive A. The current directory is B:\ and you want to use the external DOS command FORMAT. If you entered the FORMAT command, DOS would search for the command in the B:\ directory. Since the DOS external commands are found in the A:\ directory, DOS would display the following error message:

```
BAD COMMAND OR FILENAME
```

You can either prefix all external commands with a drive parameter (A:FORMAT), or you can use the PATH command to set a extended search path for DOS. Setting a extended search path tells DOS where to search for a command if the command is not found in the current directory. If you are working on a floppy-disk system, you should begin your DOS session with this command:

```
PATH A:\
```

This command instructs DOS to search the root directory on drive A for any commands you issue that DOS cannot find in the current directory. The PATH command is optional on a floppy-disk system because you could preface all DOS external commands with a drive parameter of A:. The PATH command is an absolute necessity on a hard disk because a hard disk may contain many subdirectories, and only one of those subdirectories will contain the DOS external commands. For example, your system may have the DOS external commands stored in the C:\DOS subdirectory. To set an extended search path for DOS you would enter the following command:

```
PATH C:\DOS
```

If you issued a path command of PATH C:\DOS, you could then issue any DOS external command from any subdirectory on your hard disk. If DOS could not find the command in the current directory, DOS would then search the C:\DOS subdirectory for the command. If you did not set a search path of C:\DOS, you would have to preface each DOS command with C:\DOS. In the tutorial exercises for hard-disk users, you will set a path of C:\DT because a copy of the DOS external commands has been stored in this directory. On a hard-disk computer you may want to extend the search path to more than one directory. For example, important files are often stored in the root directory of drive C (C:\). The semicolon can be used to specify a list of directories to be searched by DOS. For example, the following command will extend the search path to the C:\; root directory and to the C:\DOS subdirectory:

```
PATH C:\;C:\DOS
```

General Error Messages

Problem: This error can occur with any command. You entered a command and DOS displayed the following error message:

```
BAD COMMAND OR FILENAME
```

Solution: You misspelled a command or a filename. For example, you enter the FORMAT command as FORM. Check the spelling of the command and/or the filename. This error also occurs if you have not used the PATH command to extend the DOS search path so that DOS can find the DOS external commands.

46 Formatting Disks

Problem: This error can occur with any command. You entered a command and DOS displayed the following error message:

```
INVALID PARAMETER
```

Solution: You misspelled or omitted a parameter or option. For example, you entered the command FORMAT B:/ without specifying an option. Check the command for errors.

Terms

Bad sectors (38)
Boot record sector (39)
Cluster (39)
Cylinder (39)
Data diskette (40)
Data files (39)
Data sectors (39)
Directory (38)
File Allocation Table (FAT) (38)
FORMAT command (38)
FORMAT /4 option (42)
FORMAT /S option (41)
FORMAT /T:80/N:9 option (42)
FORMAT /V option (41)
Fragmented files (40)
LABEL command (44)
PATH command (44)
Program files (39)
Sectors (38)
System diskette (41)
Tracks (38)
VOL (Volume) command (44)
Write-protect notch (42)
Write-protect window (42)
Write-protected (42)

Review Questions

Name _____

Mastery Self-Quiz True/False

Answer T for true or F for false.

1. _F_ The directory is the table of contents of a disk.
2. _T_ The FAT is an index as to the usable areas of the disk.
3. _F_ A sector is the smallest addressable location used to store data on disk.
4. _T_ Both sides of a disk are used to store data.
5. _F_ Each sector can store 1,024 bytes of data. —— 512 by
6. _T_ A cluster is also called a cylinder.
7. _F_ Hard disks use smaller cluster sizes than floppy disks. ——>
8. _T_ Files stored in noncontiguous clusters are called fragmented files.
9. _F_ If a diskette formats with bad sectors, it should be discarded.
10. _F_ Every diskette should be formatted as a system diskette.

Mastery Self-Quiz Fill-in

1. The ___V___ command is used to display the volume label of a disk.
2. The _D J Label_ command is used to add, change, or delete a volume label. without reformat
3. The _path A:_ command sets an extended search path for DOS.
4. The _____ character can be used in a PATH command to set multiple search paths.
5. The FORMAT ___N___ option is used to add a volume label.
6. The FORMAT ___S___ option is used to create a system diskette.
7. The FORMAT ___/4___ option is used to format a double-density 5.25-inch disk in a high-density drive.
8. The FORMAT _/T:80 /N:9_ options are used to format a double-density 3.5-inch disk in a high-density drive.
9. Disks can be _write protected_ so that they cannot be over-written.
10. A _____ diskette has its entire surface reserved for data.

Discussion Questions

1. Explain the use of the /V and /S options of the FORMAT command.

   /V Format disk with volume label.
   /S Format disk a system disk

2. Explain the use to the /4, /T:80, and /N:9 options of the FORMAT command.

   /4 format 3½ disk
   720 plus a normal high density of 1.44 MB
   This disk ready need by both 720 KB drives.

3. Explain the use of the PATH command. with command
   Use to extend the search path that DOS uses to find DOS external command

48 Formatting Disks

Solving Error Messages

Enter the solution to each of these problems.

Problem: When the FORMAT command attempts to format a diskette, it displays this error message:

```
Attempted write-protect violation
Format Failure
Format another (Y/N)?
```

Solution:

Problem: After the format is complete, DOS displays the following screen:

```
Format Complete

362496 bytes total disk space
  5120 bytes in bad sectors
357376 bytes available on disk
```

Solution:

Problem: FORMAT displays this error message when it attempts to format a diskette:

```
Invalid media or Track 0 bad - disk unusable
Format Failure
Format another
```

Solution:

Problem: FORMAT display this error message when you attempt to format a diskette:

```
Drive letter must be specified
```

Solution:

Problem: FORMAT displays this error message when you attempt to format a diskette:

```
BAD COMMAND OR FILENAME
```

Solution:

Chapter Three Tutorial

Disk, Diskette, And System Types

You will use your own disk for this tutorial. Identify which of following four type of disks matches yours.

```
1. 5.25-inch double-density.
2. 5.25-inch high-density.
3. 3.5-inch double-density.
4. 3.5-inch high density.
```

The manufacturer's label on the diskette will identify diskettes as DD or double-density and HD or high-density. If a 3.5-inch diskette is not labeled, if it has a single window, it is a double-density diskette, and if it has two windows, it is a high-density diskette. There are four types of disk drives as shown in the following list:

```
1. 5.25-inch double-density drives.
2. 5.25-inch high-density drives.
3. 3.5-inch double-density drives.
4. 3.5-inch high-density drives.
```

You must ask your instructor or computer center personnel which type of system (hard or floppy) and which type of disk drive will be used to format disks in this tutorial.

```
Enter system type (hard or floppy)
Enter drive type of drive A (size and density)
Enter drive type of drive B (size and density)
(hard-disk systems may not have a drive B)
Enter diskette type (size and density)
```

If you are using a floppy disk system, you will follow the steps labeled floppy-disk users. If you are using a hard-disk system, you will follow the steps labeled hard-disk users. If you are using a hard-disk system turn to page 56, otherwise do the instructions that follow:

50 Formatting Disks

Floppy-Disk Users

Check out a DOS system disk that matches the drive A type in your system (5.25-inch double-density, 5.25-inch high-density, 3.5-inch double-density, or 3.5-inch high-density).

Inserting Disks

1. Insert the DOS system disk in drive A.
2. Insert the data disk (your disk) in drive B.

Booting DOS

1. PRESS: **<CTRL-ALT-DEL>**
2. **Type the current date and press <ENTER>**
   [If you have any problems refer back to the tips used to enter the date in the tutorial for chapter two.]
3. **Type the current time and press <ENTER>**
   [If you have any problems refer back to the tips used to enter the time in the tutorial for chapter two.]
4. DOS displays the current version of DOS being used and displays the following DOS prompt:

```
A>
```

5. TYPE: **PROMPT PG** <ENTER>
   [DOS will display the following prompt:]

```
A:\>
```

Formatting a Disk

Based on the type of drive B your system has and the type of data diskette you have, you must select the appropriate section to format your diskette:

```
(1) Matching drive and diskette density which includes the
    following:
    a. 5.25-inch double-density drive and a double-density disk.
    b. 5.25-inch high-density drive and a high-density disk.
    c. 3.5-inch double-density drive and a double-density disk.
    d. 3.5-inch high-density drive and a high-density disk.
(2) 5.25-inch high-density drive and a double-density disk.
(3) 3.5-inch high-density drive and a double-density disk.
```

You must select the correct section or your diskette will fail to format. Check with your instructor or computer center personnel if you are not sure what to do.

(1) Matching Drive and Diskette Density

You are going to format your diskette in this section. Double-density 5.25-inch diskettes will format to 362,496 bytes, high-density 5.25-inch diskettes will format to 1,213,952 bytes, double-density 3.5-inch disks will format to 730,112 bytes, and high-density 3.5-inch diskettes will format to about 1,457,664 bytes. The following displays will use a 5.25-inch double-density diskette as an example. If you have another type of diskette, your numbers will be higher.

1. TYPE: **FORMAT B:** <ENTER>
   [DOS will display the following:]

```
Insert a new diskette for drive B:
and strike ENTER when ready
```

2. PRESS: **<ENTER>**
   [DOS is now formatting the disk and it will display the head (read/write head) and the cylinder (cluster) that it is formatting. This display will range from cylinder 0 to cylinder 39 (forty tracks) for 5.25-inch double-density diskettes, and will range from cylinder 0 to cylinder 79 (eighty tracks) for 3.5-inch double-density diskettes and both types of high-density diskettes.]
3. When the format process is complete DOS will display the following report. Your numbers will be higher if you are not using a 5.25-inch double-density disk.

```
Format Complete

362496 bytes total disk space
362496 bytes available on disk

Format another (Y/N)?
```

4. TYPE: **N** <ENTER>
   [The DOS prompt of A:\> should display.]
5. If DOS displays the xxx bytes in bad sectors in your report, check with your instructor or with computer center personnel.
6. Go to the section called **Switching the Default Drive** on page 54.

52 Formatting Disks

(2) 5.25-Inch High-density Drive and Double-density disk

You are going to format your diskette in this section.

1. **TYPE: FORMAT B:/4 <ENTER>**
   [The /4 option instructs DOS to format this diskette with only forty tracks. A high-density drive 5.25-inch drive defaults to eighty tracks. You may not be able to use this diskette on another computer. DOS will display the following:]

```
Insert a new diskette for drive B:
and strike ENTER when ready
```

2. **PRESS: <ENTER>**
   [DOS is now formatting the disk and it will display the head (read/write head) and the cylinder (cluster) that it is formatting. This display will range from cylinder 0 to cylinder 39 (forty tracks) for double-density diskettes.]
3. When the format process is complete DOS will display the following report:

```
Format Complete

362496 bytes total disk space
362496 bytes available on disk

Format another (Y/N)?
```

4. **TYPE: N <ENTER>**
   [The DOS prompt of A:\> should display.]
5. If DOS displays the xxx bytes in bad sectors in your report, check with your instructor or with computer center personnel.
6. Go to the section called **Switching the Default Drive** on page 54.

(3) 3.5-Inch High-density Drive and Double-density disk

You are going to format your diskette in this section.

1. TYPE: **FORMAT B:/T:80/N:9** <ENTER>
    [The /T:80/N:9 options instructs DOS to format this diskette with eighty tracks and only nine sectors. A high-density 3.5-inch drive defaults to eighty tracks and eighteen sectors. DOS will display the following:]

```
Insert a new diskette for drive B:
and strike ENTER when ready
```

2. PRESS: **<ENTER>**
    [DOS is now formatting the disk and it will display the head (read/write head) and the cylinder (cluster) that it is formatting. This display will range from cylinder 0 to cylinder 79 (eighty tracks) for double-density diskettes.]
3. When the format process is complete DOS will display the following report:

```
Format Complete

730112 bytes total disk space
730112 bytes available on disk

Format another (Y/N)?
```

4. TYPE: **N** <ENTER>
    [The DOS prompt of A:\ > should display.]
5. If DOS displays the xxx bytes in bad sectors in your report, check with your instructor or with computer center personnel.

Switching the Default Drive

You are going to enter a command to switch the default drive. DOS defaults to the boot drive (A:) but you can switch to any other drive in your system by entering the drive letter and a colon (A: or B:).

1. TYPE: **B:** <ENTER>
   [DOS should display the following prompt:]

```
B:\>
```

2. TYPE: **A:** <ENTER>
   [DOS should display the following prompt:]

```
A:\>
```

3. TYPE: **B:** <ENTER>
   [DOS should display the following prompt:]

```
B:\>
```

LABEL Command

The LABEL command is used to change, delete, or add a volume label.

1. TYPE: **A:LABEL** <ENTER>
   [You had to type A:LABEL because LABEL is an external command and is found on the DOS disk in drive A. DOS will display the following:]

```
Volume in drive B has no label

Volume label (11 characters, ENTER for none)?
```

2. TYPE: **Your initials** <ENTER>
3. TYPE: **VOL** <ENTER>
   [DOS will display the following:]

```
Volume in drive B is {your initials}
```

Bad Command Error

1.   TYPE: **LABEL** <ENTER>
   [DOS will display the following error message:]

```
Bad command or file name
```

2.   DOS displayed this error message because you entered the external command LABEL. External commands are located in the root directory of drive A. The current default drive is drive B. DOS defaults to searching the current directory of the default drive (B:\) for external commands. DOS searched the B:\ directory for the LABEL command and did not find the command.

PATH Command

You are going to enter a PATH command to extend the DOS search path to the root directory of drive A so that you can use DOS external commands (like FORMAT and LABEL) from drive B.

1.   TYPE: **PATH A:** <ENTER>

Canceling a Command

You can cancel a command by pressing <CTRL-C>. You must press and hold the <CTRL> key and the tap the C key.

1.   TYPE: **LABEL** <ENTER>
   [DOS displays the following:]

```
Volume in drive B is {your initials}
Volume label (11 characters, ENTER for none)?
```

2.   PRESS: **<CTRL-C>**
   [DOS will display ^C, cancel the the command, and display the DOS prompt.]
3.   You have completed the tutorial for chapter three. You may go back to the beginning of the floppy-disk users section on page 50 and do it again, or you can do comprehensive problem three on page 61.

Hard-Disk Users

Check Drive A and make sure that it is empty and unlatched, or open.

Booting DOS

1. Press: **<CTRL-ALT-DEL>**
2. If the system displays the DOS system prompt of C> go to step three. If the system displays a menu, check with computer center personnel to find out how you can exit the menu to DOS.
3. TYPE: **PROMPT PG** <ENTER>
   [Your prompt should match the following:]

```
C:\DT>
```

4. If your prompt matches the C:\DT> prompt, skip to the section called PATH Command. If your prompt does not match C:\DT> you must do step five.
5. TYPE: **CD\DT** <ENTER>
   [DOS should display the following prompt:]

```
C:\DT>
```

6. If your prompt does not match the C:\DT> prompt, check with your instructor or computer center personnel and do not do any more steps until you have the C:\DT> prompt.

PATH Command

DOS defaults to a search path of the root directory on the boot drive (C:\). You are going to enter a PATH command to extend the DOS search path to include the C:\DT directory where the external commands of DOS are stored so that you can use DOS external commands (like FORMAT and LABEL) from drive A.

1. TYPE: **PATH C:\;C:\DT** <ENTER>

Formatting a Disk

Based on the type of drive A and the type of data disk, select the appropriate section to format your disk:

```
(1) Matching drive and diskette density which includes the
    following:
    a. 5.25-inch double-density drive and a double-density disk.
    b. 5.25-inch high-density drive and a high-density disk.
    c. 3.5-inch double-density drive and a double-density disk.
    d. 3.5-inch high-density drive and a high-density disk.
(2) 5.25-inch high-density drive and a double-density disk.
(3) 3.5-inch high-density drive and a double-density disk.
```

You must select the correct section or your diskette will fail to format. Check with your instructor or computer center personnel if you are not sure what to do.

(1) Matching Drive and Diskette Density

You are going to format your diskette in this section. Double-density 5.25-inch diskettes will format to 362,496 bytes, high-density 5.25-inch diskettes will format to 1,213,952 bytes, double-density 3.5-inch disks will format to 730,112 bytes, and high-density 3.5-inch diskettes will format to about 1,457,664 bytes. The following displays will use a 5.25-inch double-density diskette as an example. If you have another type of diskette, your numbers will be higher.

1. Insert your diskette in drive A.
2. TYPE: **FORMAT A:** <ENTER>
   [DOS will display the following:]

```
Insert a new diskette for drive A:
and strike ENTER when ready
```

3. PRESS: <ENTER>
   [DOS is now formatting the disk and it will display the head (read/write head) and the cylinder (cluster) that it is formatting. This display will range from cylinder 0 to cylinder 39 (forty tracks) for 5.25-inch double-density diskettes, and will range from cylinder 0 to cylinder 79 (eighty tracks) for 3.5-inch double-density diskettes and both types of high-density diskettes.]
4. When the format process is complete DOS will display the following report. Your numbers will be higher if you are not using a 5.25-inch double-density disk.

```
Format Complete

362496 bytes total disk space
362496 bytes available on disk

Format another (Y/N)?
```

5. TYPE: **N** <ENTER>
   [The DOS prompt of C:\DT> should display.]
6. If DOS displays the xxx bytes in bad sectors in your report, check with your instructor or with computer center personnel.
7. Go to the section called **Switching the Default Drive** on page 60.

58 Formatting Disks

(2) 5.25-Inch High-density Drive and Double-density disk

You are going to format your diskette in this section.

1. Insert your disk in drive A.
2. **TYPE: FORMAT A:/4** <ENTER>
   [The /4 option instructs DOS to format this diskette with only forty tracks. A high-density drive 5.25-inch drive defaults to eighty tracks. You may not be able to use this diskette on another computer. DOS will display the following:]

```
Insert a new diskette for drive A:
and strike ENTER when ready
```

3. **PRESS:** <ENTER>
   [DOS is now formatting the disk and it will display the head (read/write head) and the cylinder (cluster) that it is formatting. This display will range from cylinder 0 to cylinder 39 (forty tracks) for double-density diskettes.]
4. When the format process is complete DOS will display the following report:

```
Format Complete

362496 bytes total disk space
362496 bytes available on disk

Format another (Y/N)?
```

5. **TYPE: N** <ENTER>
   [The DOS prompt of C:\DT> should display.]
6. If DOS displays the xxx bytes in bad sectors in your report, check with your instructor or with computer center personnel.
7. Go to the section called **Switching the Default Drive** on page 60.

(3) 3.5-Inch High-density Drive and Double-density disk

You are going to format your diskette in this section.

1. Insert your disk in drive A.
2. **TYPE: FORMAT A:/T:80/N:9** <ENTER>
   [The /T:80/N:9 options instructs DOS to format this diskette with eighty tracks and only nine sectors. A high-density 3.5-inch drive defaults to eighty tracks and eighteen sectors. DOS will display the following:]

```
Insert a new diskette for drive A:
and strike ENTER when ready
```

3. **PRESS: <ENTER>**
   [DOS is now formatting the disk and it will display the head (read/write head) and the cylinder (cluster) that it is formatting. This display will range from cylinder 0 to cylinder 79 (eighty tracks) for double-density diskettes.]
4. When the format process is complete DOS will display the following report:

```
Format Complete

730112 bytes total disk space
730112 bytes available on disk

Format another (Y/N)?
```

5. **TYPE: N <ENTER>**
   [The DOS prompt of C:\DT> should display.]
6. If DOS displays the xxx bytes in bad sectors in your report, check with your instructor or with computer center personnel.

60 Formatting Disks

Switching the Default Drive

You are going to enter a command to switch the default drive. DOS defaults to the boot drive (C:) but you can switch to any other drive in your system by entering the drive letter and a colon (C: or A:).

1. TYPE: **A:** <ENTER>
    [DOS should display the following prompt:]

```
A:\>
```

2. TYPE: **C:** <ENTER>
    [DOS should display the following prompt:]

```
C:\DT>
```

3. TYPE: **A:** <ENTER>
    [DOS should display the following prompt:]

```
A:\>
```

LABEL Command

The LABEL command is used to change, delete, or add a volume label.

1. TYPE: **VER** <ENTER>
    [DOS will display the version of DOS in RAM. If you are using version 2 of DOS, you must skip this section because the LABEL command is only available in Version 3.0 or later of DOS.]
2. TYPE: **LABEL** <ENTER>
    [DOS will display the following:]

```
Volume in drive A has no label

Volume label (11 characters, ENTER for none)?
```

3. TYPE: **Your initials** <ENTER>
4. TYPE: **VOL** <ENTER>
    [DOS will display the following:]

```
Volume in drive A is {your initials}
```

Canceling a Command

The <CTRL-C> sequence cancels a command after you have pressed <ENTER> to start the command. You must press and hold the <CTRL> key and the tap the C key.

1.   TYPE: **LABEL** <ENTER>
   [DOS displays the following:]

```
Volume in drive A is {your initials}

Volume label (11 characters, ENTER for none)?
```

2.   PRESS: **<CTRL-C>**
   [DOS will display ^C, cancel the the command, and display the DOS prompt.]
3.   You have completed the tutorial for chapter three. You may go back to the beginning of the hard-disk users section on page 56 and do it again, or you can do comprehensive problem three.

Comprehensive Problem Three

1. You must be connected to a printer to do this problem.
2. Floppy-disk users should switch to drive B and hard-disk users should switch to drive A.
3. Format your disk with a volume label. Make sure you use the correct options based on the drive type and diskette type.
4. Enter a volume label of your initials.
5. Use the LABEL command to change the volume label to the first eleven characters of your last name.
6. Use the VOL command to display the volume label.
7. Print the screen.
8. Floppy-disk users match to the floppy-disk screen and hard-disk users match to the hard-disk screen.
9. Your screen should match the following screen with these exceptions:
   a. The screen assumes a 5.25-inch double-density disk and a 5.25-inch drive. If you have a high-density drive, your numbers will be higher.
   b. If you are formatting a double-density diskette in a high-density drive, your FORMAT options will be different.

62 Formatting Disks

```
B:\>format b:/v
Insert new diskette for drive B:
and strike ENTER when ready

Format complete

Volume label (11 characters, ENTER for none)? KG

    362496 bytes total disk space
    362496 bytes available on disk

Format another (Y/N)?n
B:\>label

Volume in drive B is KG

Volume label (11 characters, ENTER for none)? Gorham

B:\>vol

  Volume in drive B is GORHAM
```

Floppy-disk screen

```
A:\>format a:/v
Insert new diskette for drive A:
and strike ENTER when ready

Format complete

Volume label (11 characters, ENTER for none)? KG

    362496 bytes total disk space
    362496 bytes available on disk

Format another (Y/N)?n
A:\>label

Volume in drive A is KG

Volume label (11 characters, ENTER for none)? Gorham

A:\>vol

  Volume in drive A is GORHAM
```

Hard-disk screen

Filenames and Directories

Chapter 4

Learning Objectives

After completing chapter four you will be able to:

```
1. Define filenames and extensions.
2. Use DIR to list a directory.
3. Use <CTRL-S> or <PAUSE> to pause the screen.
4. Use DIR/P to pause a directory.
5. Use DIR/W to display a wide directory listing.
6. Use wildcards to display a selective directory listing.
7. Use input and output redirection.
8. Use the filter commands, MORE, SORT, and FIND.
```

File names

When you create a file it must be given a file name because DOS will store the file under that name. The file name consists of two parts: a filename which comes first, and an optional extension which comes second and is preceded by a period. BUDGET.91 is and example of a file name. BUDGET is the filename and .91 is the extension. If an extension is assigned to a file name, it becomes part of the file name and the full file name (BUDGET.91 rather than just BUDGET) must be used to retrieve the file. The filename cannot exceed eight characters and the extension cannot exceed three characters. If you use more than the legal amount of characters, DOS will ignore the extra characters. The filename and extension can consist of letters and numbers. Some special characters (for example, $, #, and so on) are allowed but the rules have changed with different versions of DOS. If you do not use any special characters, file name creation will be simplified. Neither the filename or the extension can include embedded blanks. For example, BUD GET is an illegal file name. Since DOS reserves some names to represent system input/output devices, these names cannot be used as filenames. The following table lists reserved system device names:

Device Name	System Device
CON	Console.
PRN	Printer.
LPT1, LPT2, LPT3	Line printer one, two, and three.
AUX1 and COM1	Serial port one.
COM2	Serial port two.
NUL	Nonexistent device.

System device names

64 Filenames and Directories

DOS created the rules used to assign file names. Since applications programs operate within DOS, the rules for assigning file names are true no matter which applications program you use. Many programs allow you to create the first eight characters and then the program generates an extension that is meaningful to that program. For example, Lotus 1-2-3 version 2 allows you to create the filenames for worksheets but the program will supply the extension of WK1 for a worksheet file. Some programs such as WordPerfect don't assign extensions to most files so you are free to supply your own extension. Filenames and extensions should be used as organizational tools. If you use meaningful filenames and extensions you will find that file management is simplified. For example, all files relating to a budget process could be named with the first six letters as BUDGET. For example, BUDGETP, BUDGETA, and BUDGETG are all files that relate to a budget. The extension could be used to designate a year as in BUDGETP.91 and BUDGETP.92. You should not use extensions that are the same as extensions used by DOS. Some common DOS extensions are listed in the following table:

Extension	DOS Translation
COM	An executable program file that can be loaded directly into memory and executed without any modifications. To execute the program type the file name (without the COM extension) and press <ENTER>. For example, the program FORMAT.COM is executed by typing FORMAT and pressing <ENTER>.
EXE	An executable program file that needs to be loaded into memory with an address modification before it can be executed. Just like COM, the extension EXE, identifies a program that may be executed by typ- the name of the program.
BAT	An executable batch file (a file containing DOS commands). The batch files, created by the user, can be executed by typing the name of the file (without the BAT extension) and pressing <ENTER>.
SYS	A system file that may only be used by DOS.
BAK	A backup file. Many programs create backup copies of files that have been saved more than the once.
OVL	An overlay file (used by large applications programs when the entire program is too large to fit into RAM).
TXT	Text or ASCII file.
$$$	A temporary file created by an application program. If any $$$ files appear in the directory listing it indicates that the program was terminated abnormally by the user or by a power failure.

Common DOS extensions

You often must give DOS the disk-drive designator (A:, B:, C:) and the file name so that DOS can locate the file. The term **file specification** or filespec is used to refer to the combination of a disk-drive designator and a file name. For example, A:FORMAT.COM is a filespec. The syntax for a command may ask for a filespec rather than a file name.

DIR Command

```
Syntax: DIR [D:][filename[.ext]] [/P] [/W]
```

The **DIR {DIRectory} command** is a DOS internal command that lists the directory section of the default disk. This listing begins with a heading that displays the volume label (if any) and the name of the disk directory that is being listed. An example of a heading is the following (assuming that B: is the default drive):

```
Volume in Drive A is SIDEREAL
Directory of B:\
```

The first line of the heading lists the volume label, if any. This disk has been assigned a label of SIDEREAL. The second line of the heading lists the directory that is being displayed. The directory being displayed in this case is B:\, the root directory of drive B. The body of the directory listing will display a vertical list of the filenames, extensions, file sizes, and the date and time the file was created or last modified. The last line of the directory listing will show a summary line that indicates the number of files stored on the disk and the number of free bytes (bytes that can be used to store information) as shown by the following display:

```
6 file(s)    298000 bytes free
```

The following display shows the complete listing displayed by the DIR command:

```
Volume in drive B is SIDEREAL
Directory of B:\
BUDGETA   90    10500   1-02-90   1:20p
BUDGETA   91    11000   1-03-91   2:43p
BUDGETA   92    12500   1-02-92   5:43p
BUDGETP   90     8000   1-04-90   1:43p
BUDGETP   91    10000   1-03-91   3:43p
BUDGETP   92    13000   1-02-92   2:43p

  6 file(s)    298000 bytes free
```

For each file the DIR command displays the filename (BUDGETA), the extension (90), the number of bytes used by the file (10500), the date, (1-02-90) and the time (1:20p) that the file was created or last modified. The period (.) is not shown as part of the extension. If there are more than twenty-three files on a disk, the directory heading and some of the filenames will scroll off the screen before you can read them. There are two ways to solve this problem. The **<CTRL-S>** key sequence is used to pause a directory listing or any computer display. Press and hold the <CTRL> key and then tap the <S> key. Press <ENTER> to continue the directory listing. The <CTRL-S> sequence sends an **interrupt signal** to cause a break in the normal sequence of a DOS command. The enhanced keyboard contains a **<PAUSE>** key that can be used in place of the <CTRL-S> key sequence.

If you are using a 386 or 486 microprocessor, you will probably not be able to send the interrupt signal fast enough to pause the listing because the listing is displayed so quickly. The **DIR /P {Directory Page} option** command displays the same information as the DIR command but pauses when the screen is full and displays the following message:

```
Strike a key when ready . . .
```

Pressing <ENTER> continues the directory display. The **DIR /W {Directory Wide} option** is the most commonly used directory option. The DIR/W command displays a horizontal list of just the filename and extension of each file so that most wide directory listings will fit on one screen. The following is an example of the listing displayed by the DIR/W command:

```
Volume in drive B is SIDEREAL
Directory of   B:\

BUDGETA   90    BUDGETA  91    BUDGETA   92   BUDGETP   90    BUDGETP   91
BUDGETP   92
        6 File(s)     298000 bytes free
```

If you are displaying a very large directory, the command DIR/P/W could be used to pause the directory at the end of each full screen. If you wanted to examine the directory information on just one file (for example, BUDGETA.91) you could enter the following command:

```
DIR BUDGETP.91
```

Wildcards

DOS commands can be made more selective when **wildcard characters** are used in filenames. Wildcards in DOS are just like wildcards in a poker game, the wildcard characters can represent any other character. Wildcards are symbols that can be used in place of known or unknown characters in filenames or extensions. The DOS manual refers to them as **global filename characters**. There are two wildcard characters, the **asterisk (*) wildcard**, representing a group of characters, and the **question mark (?) wildcard**, representing a single character. A directory command can be made more selective by using wildcards. For example, the following command would just display a directory of your budget files:

```
DIR BUDGET*
```

This command asks for a directory of all files that begin with the characters BUDGET. The asterisk tells DOS to accept any other characters following BUDGET in the filename or extension. If you know that the files you want begin with BUD but you are not sure of the next three characters, the following command could be used:

```
DIR BUD???*
```

This command asks for a directory of all files that begin with BUD, have any characters in the next three positions, and have any characters in the rest of the filename. This command would display the file BUDGETP.91 but would not display BUD.91 because the pattern BUD???* specifies at least a six-character filename. Wildcards can also be used in the extension. If you have budget files with extensions of 91 for 1991 and 92 for 1992, you can display a directory of just the 1991 files with the following command:

```
DIR BUDGET*.91
```

The following command would list just those files with an extension of COM:

```
DIR *.COM
```

Wildcards can be used with many DOS command, not just the DIR command. Only one asterisk can be used in the filename and only one can be used in the extension because the asterisk specifies that any character can occupy that position and any remaining positions in the filename and extension. Multiple question marks can be used but question marks should not follow an asterisk in a filename or an extension.

Directory Error Messages

Problem: The DIR command reads the directory of the disk but displays the following message:

```
File not Found
```

Solution: the directory does not contain any files or it contains no filenames that match the wildcard pattern that you specified. Check the wildcard pattern for errors.

Problem: The DIR command is unable to read the directory of the disk in drive A and displays the following error message:

```
General Failure error reading drive A
Abort, Retry, Fail?
```

Solution: The disk may not be formatted or you may be attempting to read a high-density disk in a double-density drive. Check the disk and if it is the correct density for the drive, type R to retry the command, but if you receive the same error message, type A to abort the command and return to the system prompt.

DOS Editing Keys

You will often make a small error when you enter a DOS command. The **DOS editing keys** can be used to retrieve and change the last DOS command entered, so that the command can be entered again without duplicating the keystrokes. DOS captures the last command entered in an area called the **input buffer**. The DOS editing keys are used to display the command stored in the input buffer and edit that command. The DOS editing keys are summarized in the following table:

Editing Key	Function
<F1>	Display one character at a time from the buffer.
<F3>	Display all characters in the buffer.
<DEL>	Delete one character from the buffer.
<INS>	Insert characters at cursor location.
<ESC>	Cancel the operation.

DOS editing keys

For example, the last DOS command entered was DIR/P. You want to enter the DIR/W command. You would press <F3> which will display the DIR/P command on the screen. Press <BACKSPACE> once to erase the P, type W, and the press <ENTER>. In another example, the last command entered was DIR/W B:*.COM and you want to enter the command DIR/W A:*.COM. You would press <F1> six times to display the command up to the drive designator (B). Then you would press <INS>, type the A, press <INS> again, press <DEL> to delete the B, and then press <F3> to display the rest of the command.

Redirection

The standard input device is the keyboard and the standard output device is the screen. **Redirection** involves changing the standard input device or standard output device used by a DOS command to another input or output device. The less than symbol (<) is used as an **input redirection operator** and directs DOS to accept input from a source other than the keyboard. The greater than symbol (>) is used as an **output redirection operator** and directs DOS to send the output of a command to a device other than the screen. The most common use of this technique is to redirect output from the screen to the printer. For example, the DIR command will display its output on the screen. The following command redirects the output of the DIR command to the printer:

```
DIR > PRN
```

The output of the DIR command will not be displayed on the screen, it will be displayed on the printer. PRN is the DOS system-device name for the printer.

Filter Commands

Filter commands can be used to take standard DOS output, modify it in some way, and then send it to the standard output device. **Piping** is another term commonly applied to this procedure. DOS sends information through a pipe from a command to the standard output device (the screen). Filter commands work like a filter attached to DOS's piping system. The filter commands receive the input from the pipe, alter the information and then send it to the standard output device through the pipe. The first command outputs to a temporary pipe file that is read by the second command. If filtering requires many operations, multiple temporary pipe files are created by DOS. When the filtering operation is completed, DOS deletes the temporary pipe files. The **filter symbol** is the ,"|", or split vertical line symbol. The filter commands are DOS utility programs that are stored with the DOS external commands on the DOS disk or in the DOS directory. The following table summarizes the three filter commands provided by DOS:

Filter	Function
MORE	Displays 23 lines on screen, and waits for a keystroke.
SORT	Sorts information into a desired sequence.
FIND	Searches a file for a specified character string.

Filter commands

MORE Filter

```
Syntax: Command | MORE or [D:]MORE < [D:]filename[.ext]
```

The **MORE filter command** is used to display a full screen of output and then pause until a key is pressed. The following command will display a directory listing on the screen, twenty-three lines at a time:

```
DIR | MORE
```

The output from the first program (DIR), becomes input to the second program (MORE). This command is superior to the DIR/P command because the directory heading will not scroll off the screen. MORE.COM is a filter program which manipulates a stream of characters coming from the standard input and sends the altered information to the standard output device. The MORE filter command displays the first twenty-three lines of information on the screen and then displays --More-- at the bottom of the screen. You can press <ENTER> to continue to the next screenful. The MORE filter can be used whenever you have a sizable amount of information to display and you wish to read the current screen and then continue. The MORE filter can be combined with input redirection. The following command will display the file LARGE.TXT on the screen, one screenful at a time:

```
MORE < B:LARGE.TXT
```

The MORE filter will create some temporary files that may display as 02111E23 and 0211F23 OR %PIPE1.$$$ and %PIPE2.$$$ depending upon whether you have version 2 or version 3 of DOS. These temporary files are created at the root directory. DOS will delete these temporary files when the MORE command is completed.

SORT Filter

```
Syntax: Command | SORT [/R] [/+N] or [D:]SORT [/R] [/+N]
[D:]filename[.ext]
```

You may have noticed that a directory listing generated by the DIR command is not in alphabetical order. The **DIR | SORT** command is used to display an ordered directory. The **SORT filter command** filters the directory listing through the DOS SORT program. The SORT.EXE DOS utility program arranges lines of inputted to it and sends the sorted information to the standard output device (the screen). If SORT is used with no parameters, it will sort the input in ascending ASCII order from lowest to highest (special characters sort first, followed by numbers, followed by letters) starting in the first column of the display (filename). The SORT command is not case-sensitive, for example, uppercase A and lowercase a will be sorted as they occur in the filename. The following command will create a directory listing in ascending order by filename:

```
DIR | SORT
```

The following command, using the /R option, sorts the directory in reverse ASCII order (descending order, from highest to lowest):

```
DIR | SORT /R
```

The /+N option uses an **offset value** to sort the directory on some column other than the default of filename. The following table shows the offset values that can be used with the /+N option:

Offset Value	Sorts by
1	File name (default)
10	Extension
14	File size
24	File date
34	File time

SORT offset values

The following command will display a directory listing sorted on extension:

```
DIR | SORT /+10
```

The directory will only be sorted on the screen, not on the disk, so this command has to be reissued each time you wish to display a sorted directory. You can combine two filtering commands as shown in the following command which will sort the directory and then display it on the screen, twenty-three lines at a time:

```
DIR | SORT | MORE
```

You can combine a filter command with an output redirection command as shown by the following command which will sort the directory and then print the sorted directory:

```
DIR | SORT > PRN
```

FIND Filter

```
Syntax: [D:]FIND "Text" [D:]filename[.ext]
```

The **FIND Filter** command is used to search a file for a specified character string. The character string must be enclosed in quotes. The FIND filter is case-sensitive which means that the case of the specified character string must match the case of the character string found in the file. The following command uses the FIND filter to display a directory listing of all files that have a creation date of 12-31-91:

```
DIR | FIND "12-31-91"
```

Redirection Error Message

Problem: You have entered a redirection command and DOS displays the following error message:

```
FILE CREATION ERROR
```

Solution: You issued the command without giving DOS a device to redirect the output to. For example, you entered the command DIR > without indicating that PRN should be the device.

Terms

Asterisk (*) wildcard (66)
DIR /P {Directory Page} option (66)
DIR /W {Directory Wide} option (66)
DIR {DIRectory} command (65)
DIR | SORT (70)
DOS editing keys (68)
File specification (64)
Filter commands (65)
Filter symbol (69)
FIND Filter command (71)
Global filename characters (66)
Input buffer (68)
Input redirection operator (68)
Interrupt signal (65)
MORE filter command (69)
Offset value (70)
Output redirection operator (68)
Piping (69)
Question mark (?) wildcard (66)
Redirection (68)
SORT filter command (70)
Wildcard characters (66)
<CTRL-S> (65)
<PAUSE> (65)

Review Questions

Name _____

Mastery Self-Quiz True/False

Answer T for true or F for false.

1. ___ An extension cannot exceed eight characters in length.
2. ___ CON should not be used as a filename.
3. ___ Embedded blanks can be used in a filename.
4. ___ Filespec is a combination of a disk drive designator and a file name.
5. ___ The DIR command displays the amount of free bytes on a disk.
6. ___ DIR/W is the most commonly used directory command.
7. ___ DIR *.BAT will list all files that have an extension of .BAT.
8. ___ DIR BUDGET.91 will list the directory information for the file BUDGET.91.
9. ___ DIR BUD???.* will list all files that begin with BUD.
10. ___ Question mark wildcards should not follow an asterisk wildcard in the filename or extension.

Mastery Self-Quiz Fill-in

1. The file name consists of a _____ and an optional _____.
2. _____ is the extension of a backup file.
3. The DIR _____ option pauses the screen display.
4. The DIR _____ option displays a wide directory.
5. The command _____ will display all files with an extension of EXE.
6. The command _____ will sort the directory in reverse order on the extension.
7. The _____ wildcard can represent a group of characters.
8. The _____ wildcard can represent a single character.
9. The command _____ will redirect the output of the DIR command to the printer.
10. The command _____ will use the MORE filter to display a directory twenty-three lines at a time.

Discussion Questions

1. Explain the use of the /P and /W options of the DIR command.

2. Give examples of using the * wildcard and the ? wildcard in directory commands.

3. Discuss the use of the three filter commands.

74 Filenames and Directories

Solving Error Messages

Enter the solution to each of these problems.

Problem: The DIR command reads the directory of the disk but displays the following message:

```
File not Found
```

Solution:

Problem: The DIR command is unable to read the directory of the disk in drive A and displays the following error message:

```
General Failure error reading drive A
Abort, Retry, Fail?
```

Solution:

Problem: You have entered a redirection command and DOS displays the following error message:

```
FILE CREATION ERROR
```

Solution:

Chapter Four Tutorial

If you are using a floppy-disk system, you will follow the steps labeled floppy-disk users. If you are using a hard-disk system, you will follow the steps labeled hard-disk users. If you are using a hard-disk system turn to page 80, otherwise do the instructions that follow.

Floppy-Disk Users

1. Insert the DOS system disk in drive A and insert the data disk in drive B.
2. Do a warm boot and enter the date and time.
3. TYPE: **PATH A:** <ENTER>
4. TYPE: **PROMPT PG** <ENTER>
   [DOS will display the following prompt:]

```
A:\>
```

DIR/P Command

1. TYPE: **DIR/P** <ENTER>
   [Your screen should match the following (the screen will not match exactly unless you are using Version 3.3 of DOS):]

```
COMMAND    COM     25276    1-08-88    1:43p
ANSI       SYS      1647    1-08-88    1:43p
APPEND     EXE      5794    1-08-88    1:43p
ASSIGN     COM      1530    1-08-88    1:43p
ATTRIB     EXE     10656    1-08-88    1:43p
CHKDSK     COM      9819    1-08-88    1:43p
COMP       COM      4183    1-08-88    1:43p
COUNTRY    SYS     11254    1-08-88    1:43p
DISKCOMP   COM      5848    1-08-88    1:43p
DISKCOPY   COM      6264    1-08-88    1:43p
DISPLAY    SYS     11259    1-08-88    1:43p
DRIVER     SYS      1165    1-08-88    1:43p
EDLIN      COM      7495    1-08-88    1:43p
EXE2BIN    EXE      3050    1-08-88    1:43p
FASTOPEN   EXE      3888    1-08-88    1:43p
FDISK      COM     48919    1-08-88    1:43p
FIND       EXE      6403    1-08-88    1:43p
FORMAT     COM     11671    1-08-88    1:43p
GRAFTABL   COM      6136    1-08-88    1:43p
GRAPHICS   COM     13943    1-08-88    1:43p
JOIN       EXE      9612    1-08-88    1:43p
KEYB       COM      9041    1-08-88    1:43p
LABEL      COM      2346    1-08-88    1:43p
Strike a key when ready . . .
```

76 Filenames and Directories

2.   PRESS: **<ENTER>**
   [You pressed <ENTER> to continue the directory display. DOS will display the rest of the files, and then the A> DOS prompt will appear.]
3.   TYPE: **CLS** <ENTER>

DIR/W Command

1.   TYPE: **DIR/W** <ENTER>
   [Your screen should match the following (if you are using a version other than 3.3 the screen will not match exactly but the format of the screen will match):]

```
Volume in drive A has no label
Directory of  A:\

COMMAND  COM   ANSI     SYS   APPEND   EXE   ASSIGN   COM   ATTRIB   EXE
CHKDSK   COM   COMP     COM   COUNTRY  SYS   DISKCOMP COM   DISKCOPY COM
DISPLAY  SYS   DRIVER   SYS   EDLIN    COM   EXE2BIN  EXE   FASTOPEN EXE
FDISK    COM   FIND     EXE   FORMAT   COM   GRAFTABL COM   GRAPHICS COM
JOIN     EXE   KEYB     COM   LABEL    COM   MODE     COM   MORE     COM
NLSFUNC  EXE   PRINT    COM   RECOVER  COM   SELECT   COM   SORT     EXE
SUBST    EXE   SYS      COM   TREE     COM
       33 File(s)        19456 bytes free
```

2.   TYPE: **CLS** <ENTER>

Wildcards

The two wildcards, * (asterisk) and ? (question mark), can be used to display selective directory listings.

1.   TYPE: **DIR DIS?*.*** <ENTER>
   [You asked DOS to display a directory listing of all files that begin with DIS, have any character in position four of the filename, and have any characters in the rest of the filename and extension. DOS should display the following directory listing (depending upon the type of disk you are using the number of bytes free may be higher):]

```
Volume in drive A has no label
Directory of  A:\

DISKCOMP COM      5848   1-08-88
DISKCOPY COM      6264   1-08-88
DISPLAY  SYS     11259   1-08-88
        3 File(s)        19456 bytes free
```

2.   TYPE: **CLS** <ENTER>
3.   TYPE: **DIR DISK*.*** <ENTER>
   [You asked DOS to display a directory listing of all files that begin with DISK and have any characters in the rest of the filename and extension. DOS should list the following files:]

```
DISKCOMP  COM        5848    1-08-88
DISKCOPY  COM        6264    1-08-88
```

4. TYPE: **CLS** <ENTER>
5. TYPE: **DIR/W *.SYS** <ENTER>
   [You asked DOS to display a directory listing of any files that have an SYS extension. The /W option is used to just display the file names. DOS should list the following files:]

```
ANSI      SYS      COUNTRY   SYS      DISPLAY   SYS      DRIVER    SYS
```

6. TYPE: **CLS** <ENTER>

Using the DOS Editing Keys

The DOS editing keys can be use to retrieve the last command entered, modify the command, and issue the modified command. Make sure that <NUM LOCK> is toggled off.

1. TYPE: **DIR/W *.SYS** <ENTER>
   [DOS displays files with an extension of SYS.]
2. PRESS: **<F3>**
   *[DOS displays the last command of DIR/W *.SYS.]*
3. PRESS: **<BACKSPACE> three times**
   [You have erased the SYS portion of the command.]
4. TYPE: **COM** <ENTER>
   *[You have changed the command to DIR/W *.COM. DOS should list all files with COM extensions.]*
5. PRESS: **<F1> four times**
   [The <F1> key displays the previous command one character at a time. Your screen should display the following on the DOS command line:]

```
DIR/
```

6. PRESS: **<INS>**
   [You have toggled on the insert mode so that you can insert characters into a command.]
7. PRESS: **P**
   [You have inserted the P {Page} option.]
8. PRESS: **<DEL>**
   [You have deleted the W {Wide} option.]
9. PRESS: **<F3>**
   [Pressing <F3> displays the rest of the command. Your command should match the following:]

```
DIR/P *.COM
```

78 Filenames and Directories

10.   PRESS: <ENTER>
[All files with a COM extension will be displayed with the /P option rather than the /W option.]

Using Filter Commands

The filter commands MORE and SORT can be used to modify the output of DIR commands.

1. **Unwrite-protect the DOS disk. Check with computer center personnel if you don't know how to do this step.**
2. TYPE: **CLS** <ENTER>
3. TYPE: **DIR/P** <ENTER>
   [Note that the heading that shows the volume label and the directory displayed scrolls off the screen.]
4. PRESS <ENTER>
5. TYPE: **CLS** <ENTER>
6. TYPE: **DIR | MORE** <ENTER>
   [The MORE filter will display twenty-three lines on the screen and displays --More-- at the bottom of the screen. Unlike the DIR/P command, the heading that shows the volume label, and the directory displayed will not scroll off the screen. Two temporary files created by the MORE command will be displayed. The files are deleted by DOS when the command is completed. Your first screen should match the following:]

```
 Volume in drive A has no label
 Directory of A:\

COMMAND    COM    25276   1-08-88
ANSI       SYS     1647   1-08-88
APPEND     EXE     5794   1-08-88
ASSIGN     COM     1530   1-08-88
ATTRIB     EXE    10656   1-08-88
CHKDSK     COM     9819   1-08-88
COMP       COM     4183   1-08-88
COUNTRY    SYS    11254   1-08-88
DISKCOMP   COM     5848   1-08-88
DISKCOPY   COM     6264   1-08-88
DISPLAY    SYS    11259   1-08-88
DRIVER     SYS     1165   1-08-88
EDLIN      COM     7495   1-08-88
EXE2BIN    EXE     3050   1-08-88
FASTOPEN   EXE     3888   1-08-88
FDISK      COM    48919   1-08-88
FIND       EXE     6403   1-08-88
FORMAT     COM    11671   1-08-88
GRAFTABL   COM     6136   1-08-88
GRAPHICS   COM    13943   1-08-88
-- More --
```

7. Notice that COMMAND.COM is not in alphabetical order.
8. PRESS: <ENTER>
   [You pressed <ENTER> to continue the directory display.]
9. TYPE: **CLS** <ENTER>

10. TYPE: **DIR | SORT | MORE** <ENTER>
    [The SORT filter has been used to sort the directory on the default of filename. The COMMAND.COM file will now be sorted in correct alphabetical sequence. The MORE filter displays the output twenty-three lines at a time. The first two files are piping files and will differ with each system. These files are deleted at the end of the process. Your first screen should match the following:]

```
 Directory of A:\
  Volume in drive A has no label

02171B5C                    0     1-04-92
02171D02                    0     1-04-92
ANSI        SYS          1647     1-08-88
APPEND      EXE          5794     1-08-88
ASSIGN      COM          1530     1-08-88
ATTRIB      EXE         10656     1-08-88
CHKDSK      COM          9819     1-08-88
COMMAND     COM         25276     1-08-88
COMP        COM          4183     1-08-88
COUNTRY     SYS         11254     1-08-88
DISKCOMP    COM          5848     1-08-88
DISKCOPY    COM          6264     1-08-88
DISPLAY     SYS         11259     1-08-88
DRIVER      SYS          1165     1-08-88
EDLIN       COM          7495     1-08-88
EXE2BIN     EXE          3050     1-08-88
FASTOPEN    EXE          3888     1-08-88
FDISK       COM         48919     1-08-88
FIND        EXE          6403     1-08-88
-- More --
```

11. PRESS: <ENTER>
12. **Write-protect the DOS disk. Check with computer center personnel if you don't know how to do this step.**
13. You have completed the tutorial for chapter four. You can go back to the beginning of the floppy-disk section on page 75 and do the tutorial again, or you can do comprehensive problem four on page 83.

80 Filenames and Directories

Hard-Disk Users

1. Insert your data disk in drive A.
2. Do a warm boot.
3. TYPE: **PROMPT PG** <ENTER>
4. TYPE: **PATH C:\;C:\DT** <ENTER>
5. TYPE: **CD\DT** <ENTER>
   [DOS should display the following prompt:]

```
C:\DT>
```

6. If your prompt does not match the C:\DT> prompt, check with your instructor or computer center personnel and do not do any more steps until you have the C:\DT> prompt.

Wildcards

The two wildcards, * (asterisk) and ? (question mark), can be used to display selective directory listings.

1. TYPE: **DIR DIS?*.*** <ENTER>
   [You asked DOS to display a directory listing of all files that begin with DIS, have any character in position four of the filename, and have any characters in the rest of the filename and extension. DOS should display the following directory listing (depending upon the type of disk you are using, the number of bytes free may be higher):]

```
Volume in drive C has no label
Directory of   C:\DT

DISKCOMP COM       5848    1-08-88
DISKCOPY COM       6264    1-08-88
DISPLAY  SYS      11259    1-08-88
        3 File(s)      19456 bytes free
```

2. TYPE: **CLS** <ENTER>
3. TYPE: **DIR DISK*.*** <ENTER>
   [You asked DOS to display a directory listing of all files that begin with DISK and have any characters in the rest of the filename and extension. DOS should list the following files:]

```
DISKCOMP COM       5848    1-08-88
DISKCOPY COM       6264    1-08-88
```

4. TYPE: **CLS** <ENTER>
5. TYPE: **DIR/W *.SYS** <ENTER>
   [You asked DOS to display a directory listing of any files that have an SYS extension. The /W option was used to just display the file names. DOS should list the following files:]

```
| ANSI   SYS    COUNTRY  SYS    DISPLAY  SYS    DRIVER  SYS |
```

6.   TYPE: **CLS** <ENTER>

Using the DOS Editing Keys

The DOS editing keys can be use to retrieve the last command entered, modify the command, and issue the modified command. Make sure that <NUM LOCK> is toggled off.

1. TYPE: **DIR/W *.SYS** <ENTER>
   [DOS displays files with an extension of SYS.]
2. PRESS: **<F3>**
   *[DOS displays the last command of DIR/W *.SYS.]*
3. PRESS: **<BACKSPACE> three times**
   [You have erased the SYS portion of the command.]
4. TYPE: **COM** <ENTER>
   *[You have changed the command to DIR/W *.COM. DOS should list all files with COM extensions.]*
5. PRESS: **<F1> four times**
   [The <F1> key displays the previous command one character at a time. Your screen should display the following on the DOS command line:]

```
DIR/
```

6. PRESS: **<INS>**
   [You have toggled on the insert mode so that you can insert characters into a command.]
7. PRESS: **P**
   [You have inserted the P {Page} option.]
8. PRESS: **<DEL>**
   [You have deleted the W {Wide} option.]
9. PRESS: **<F3>**
   [Pressing <F3> displays the rest of the command. Your command should match the following:]

```
DIR/P *.COM
```

10. PRESS: **<ENTER>**
    [All files with a COM extension will be displayed with the /P option rather than the /W option.]

Using Filter Commands

The filter commands MORE and SORT can be used to modify the output of DIR commands.

1. TYPE: **CLS** <ENTER>
2. TYPE: **DIR/P** <ENTER>
   [Note that the heading that shows the volume label and the directory displayed scrolls off the screen.]
3. PRESS: **<ENTER>**

82 Filenames and Directories

4. TYPE: **CLS** <ENTER>
5. TYPE: **DIR | MORE** <ENTER>
    [The MORE filter will display twenty-three lines on the screen and displays --More-- at the bottom of the screen. Unlike the DIR/P command, the heading that shows the volume label and the directory displayed will not scroll off the screen. The first two files are directory files created by DOS. Your first screen should match the following:]

```
Volume in drive C has no label
Directory of C:\DT

.              <DIR>        1-01-92
..             <DIR>        1-01-92
COMMAND  COM    25276       1-08-88
ANSI     SYS     1647       1-08-88
APPEND   EXE     5794       1-08-88
ASSIGN   COM     1530       1-08-88
ATTRIB   EXE    10656       1-08-88
CHKDSK   COM     9819       1-08-88
COMP     COM     4183       1-08-88
COUNTRY  SYS    11254       1-08-88
DISKCOMP COM     5848       1-08-88
DISKCOPY COM     6264       1-08-88
DISPLAY  SYS    11259       1-08-88
DRIVER   SYS     1165       1-08-88
EDLIN    COM     7495       1-08-88
EXE2BIN  EXE     3050       1-08-88
FASTOPEN EXE     3888       1-08-88
FDISK    COM    48919       1-08-88
FIND     EXE     6403       1-08-88
FORMAT   COM    11671       1-08-88
-- More --
```

6. Notice that COMMAND.COM is not in alphabetical order.
7. PRESS: **<ENTER>**
    [You pressed <ENTER> to continue the directory display.]
8. TYPE: **CLS** <ENTER>
9. TYPE: **DIR | SORT | MORE** <ENTER>
    [The SORT filter has been used to sort the directory on the default of filename. The COMMAND.COM file will now be sorted in correct alphabetical sequence. The MORE filter displays the output twenty-three lines at a time. The first two files are directory files created by DOS. Your first screen should match the following:]

```
Directory of C:\DT
Volume in drive C has no label
.              <DIR>         1-01-92
..             <DIR>         1-01-92
ANSI     SYS     1647        1-08-88
APPEND   EXE     5794        1-08-88
ASSIGN   COM     1530        1-08-88
ATTRIB   EXE    10656        1-08-88
CHKDSK   COM     9819        1-08-88
COMMAND  COM    25276        1-08-88
COMP     COM     4183        1-08-88
COUNTRY  SYS    11254        1-08-88
DISKCOMP COM     5848        1-08-88
DISKCOPY COM     6264        1-08-88
DISPLAY  SYS    11259        1-08-88
DRIVER   SYS     1165        1-08-88
EDLIN    COM     7495        1-08-88
EXE2BIN  EXE     3050        1-08-88
FASTOPEN EXE     3888        1-08-88
FDISK    COM    48919        1-08-88
FIND     EXE     6403        1-08-88
-- More --
```

9.   PRESS: <ENTER>
10.   You have completed the tutorial for chapter four. You can go back to the beginning of the hard disk section on page 80 and do the tutorial again, or you can do comprehensive problem four.

Comprehensive Problem Four

Only the files will be shown in the displays. Floppy-disk users should have a current directory of A:\ and the data disk should be in drive B. Hard-disk users should have a current directory of C:\DT and the data disk should be in drive A.

1. Your diskette should have a volume label of the first eleven characters or your last name. If it does not have this label, use the LABEL command to add it.
2. Clear the screen.
3. Use the DIR command to display a directory of the COMMAND.COM file. The file on your screen should match the following:

```
COMMAND  COM    25276    1-08-88
```

4. Use the DIR/W command to display all files that begin with DIS. The files on your screen should match the following:

84 Filenames and Directories

```
DISKCOMP COM      DISKCOPY COM      DISPLAY  SYS
```

5. Use the DIR/W command to display all files that have an extension of .SYS. The files on your screen should match the following:

```
ANSI     SYS      COUNTRY  SYS      DISPLAY  SYS      DRIVER   SYS
```

6. Print the screen. Your screen should match the following (only the files are shown, your screen will show prompts, commands, and volume label information):

```
COMMAND  COM      25276    1-08-88

DISKCOMP COM      DISKCOPY COM      DISPLAY  SYS

ANSI     SYS      COUNTRY  SYS      DISPLAY  SYS      DRIVER   SYS
```

7. Use the redirection operator to print a wide directory. Floppy-disk users should match to the floppy-disk screen and hard-disk users should match to the hard-disk screen. Your printout should match the following (only the files are shown):

```
COMMAND  COM   ANSI     SYS   APPEND   EXE   ASSIGN   COM   ATTRIB   EXE
CHKDSK   COM   COMP     COM   COUNTRY  SYS   DISKCOMP COM   DISKCOPY COM
DISPLAY  SYS   DRIVER   SYS   EDLIN    COM   EXE2BIN  EXE   FASTOPEN EXE
FDISK    COM   FIND     EXE   FORMAT   COM   GRAFTABL COM   GRAPHICS COM
JOIN     EXE   KEYB     COM   LABEL    COM   MODE     COM   MORE     COM
NLSFUNC  EXE   PRINT    COM   RECOVER  COM   SELECT   COM   SORT     EXE
SUBST    EXE   SYS      COM   TREE     COM
```

Floppy-disk users screen

```
.                          COMMAND  COM  ANSI     SYS  APPEND   EXE
ASSIGN   COM  ATTRIB   EXE  CHKDSK   COM  COMP     COM  COUNTRY  SYS
DISKCOMP COM  DISKCOPY COM  DISPLAY  SYS  DRIVER   SYS  EDLIN    COM
EXE2BIN  EXE  FASTOPEN EXE  FDISK    COM  FIND     EXE  FORMAT   COM
GRAFTABL COM  GRAPHICS COM  JOIN     EXE  KEYB     COM  LABEL    COM
MODE     COM  MORE     COM  NLSFUNC  EXE  PRINT    COM  RECOVER  COM
SELECT   COM  SORT     EXE  SUBST    EXE  SYS      COM  TREE     COM
```

Hard-disk users screen

8. Turn in both printouts.

File Manipulation

Chapter 5

Learning Objectives

After completing chapter five you will be able to:

```
1.  Use COPY to make copies of existing files.
2.  Use XCOPY to make selective copies of existing files.
3.  Use DISKCOPY to make a copy of a diskette.
4.  Use REN to rename files.
5.  Use DEL to erase files.
6.  Use ATTRIB to give a file read-only status.
7.  Use CHKDSK to display disk and RAM status reports.
```

COPY Command

```
Syntax: COPY [D:]<Source File Name> [D:][Target File Name]   [/V]
```

The **COPY command** is a DOS internal command used to make duplicate copies of existing files. COPY is primarily used to transfer a file or files from one disk to another. This command is also used to make a **backup** of a single file, a number of files, an entire diskette, or a directory on a hard disk. A backup file is a copy of a file that can be used if the original file is destroyed. The following is an example of the COPY command:

```
COPY A:FILE1 B:FILE2
```

In the above example A:FILE1 is the source filespec (the source drive and source file name of the file to be copied) and B:FILE2 is the target file filespec (the target drive and target file name to be copied to). You must leave a space between the source filespec and the target filespec. The above command will create a new file on drive B called FILE2 that has the same contents as FILE1 on drive A. If a file named FILE2 (the target file) existed on drive B prior to using the COPY command, the COPY command would overwrite this file without warning the user. If the COPY command successfully copies a file, DOS will display the following message:

```
1 File(s) copied
```

86 File Manipulation

If you copy more than one file, DOS will list each file name as it copies the files. If you use the COPY command but do not provide a source-drive parameter, DOS will use the default drive. Assume that the default drive is A, and you issued the following command:

```
COPY FILE1 B:FILE2
```

DOS will copy FILE1 from drive A to drive B and assign the file name of FILE2 to the copied file. If you use the COPY command and you do not provide a target file name, DOS will assign the file name used on the source drive. An example of this type of COPY command is the following command:

```
COPY FILE1 B:
```

Wildcard characters can be used with the COPY command to make a selective copy. For example, the default drive is drive A and you issued the following command:

```
COPY FIL?1 B:
```

This command would copy any files on drive A that begin with FIL, have any character in position four of the filename, and have the character 1 in position five of the filename. For example, FILE1, FILT1, and FILQ1 would be copied to drive B, but FILE2 and FILE1Q would not be copied. FILE1Q would not be copied because the wildcard pattern FIL?1 only provides for five positions in the filename. Multiple ? wildcards can be used, such as a pattern of FIL??. Assume that drive A is the default drive and the following COPY command was issued:

```
COPY FIL* B:
```

This command would copy any files on drive A that begin with FIL. For example, the files FILE1, FILT1, FILQ1, FILE2, and FILE1Q would be copied to drive B, but the file FIQE would not be copied. The COPY command can be used to do the following:

```
1. Copy a file onto the same disk with a different name.
   Example: COPY FILE1 FILE2
2. Copy a file from one disk to another disk.
   Example: COPY C:FILE1 A:FILE1
3. Copy a file from one disk to another disk and change the
   name of the file.
   Example: COPY C:FILE1 A:FILE2
4. Copy several files from one disk to another disk.
   Example: COPY C:BA*.* A:
5. Copy all files from one disk or directory to another disk.
   Example: COPY C:*.* A:
```

COPY *.*

The most powerful COPY command is the **COPY *.* command** which tells DOS to copy files that have any filename (the first * substitutes for any filename) and any extension (the second * substitutes for any extension). The COPY *.* command should be used periodically to make **backup diskettes** of important files. A backup diskette is a disk that can be used if the original disk fails. COPY *.* can be used to copy a portion of the hard disk to a floppy disk. The BACKUP command, discussed in chapter eight, is typically used to completely backup a hard disk to floppy disk. COPY *.* can also be used to unfragment a floppy disk by copying it to another floppy disk. The **COPY /V (Verify) option** can be added to any COPY command to make DOS double check the copy for accuracy. Using the /V option will double the amount of time used to make a copy.

COPY Errors

Problem: You enter a COPY command and DOS displays the following error message:

```
File cannot be copied onto itself
   0 File(s) copied
```

Solution: You have entered a command to copy a file without specifying a target drive. For example, you entered the command COPY BUDGET.91. DOS will not overwrite a file on the same disk. You can solve this problem by specifying a target disk drive (COPY BUDGET.91 B:) or specifying a target file name to copy the file on the same drive (COPY BUDGET.91 BUDGETB.91).

Problem: You enter a COPY command and DOS displays the following error message:

```
Insufficient disk space, 0 file(s) copied.
```

Solution: The disk that you are copying to is full. You must either erase one or more files from the target disk or use another disk. If you are copying multiple files, the COPY command may copy some of the files (it lists each file name as it is copied) and then halt and display the insufficient disk space error as the disk is filled up. You will have erase some files on the target disk or use another disk.

XCOPY Command

```
Syntax: XCOPY <Source filespec> [Target filespec> [/W] [/P]
[/D:mm-dd-yy] [/S] [/E]
```

The **XCOPY command** is an external DOS command that can be used to copy selected files. This command has options that can interactively select or reject the name of each file to be copied. XCOPY also has an option that can be used to selectively copy files based on a specified date. XCOPY was introduced in Version 3.2 of DOS. The following is an example of an XCOPY command that will allow the user to select or reject the name of each file to be copied from a group of files:

```
XCOPY A: B:/W/P
```

The **XCOPY /W (Wait) option** instructs DOS to display the following message before copying any files:

```
Press any key to begin copying files
```

You must press <ENTER> to begin copying files and the **XCOPY /P (Prompt) option** instructs DOS to prompt you with a (Y/N)? after displaying each file name on the source drive. If you type Y and press <ENTER> the file will be copied to the target drive and then the next file will be displayed with the (Y/N)? prompt. If you type N and press <ENTER> the file displayed will not be copied but the next file name will be displayed with the (Y/N)? prompt. You could also use wildcards with the XCOPY command to restrict the files that would be copied from one drive to another. The following command using the **XCOPY /D (Date) option** will selectively copy files on the basis of a specified date:

```
XCOPY A: B:/D:12-31-92
```

This command will copy to drive B any files on drive A that have a creation or modification date of equal to or greater than 12-31-92. For example, a file dated 12-06-92 will be not be copied but a file dated 12-31-92 will be copied. The format of the date option is /D:mm-dd-yy where mm indicates the month (01 through 12), dd indicates the day (01 through 31), and yy indicates the year (80 through 99). The /W and /P options could also be used in combination with the /D option. The /S and /E options will be discussed in chapter six.

DISKCOPY Command

```
Syntax: [D:]DISKCOPY <Source Drive> <Target Drive>
```

The **DISKCOPY command** is a DOS external command used to copy the entire contents of one floppy diskette to another floppy diskette. The only time that DISKCOPY should be used instead of COPY *.* is when you are copying a disk that contains hidden files (such as the DOS system disk). DISKCOPY makes a complete copy including hidden files while COPY *.* does not copy hidden files. The DISKCOPY command cannot be used to unfragment a diskette because it makes an exact duplicate of the disk with the fragmented files intact. If the source and target diskettes are different types of diskettes (for example, drive A is a high density drive and drive B is a double-density drive), the DISKCOPY command will display an error message and refuse to make the copy. DISKCOPY cannot be used to copy to or from a hard drive. The following command will copy the diskette in drive A to the diskette in drive B:

```
DISKCOPY A: B:
```

If the target diskette is not formatted or has a different format type than the source diskette, DISKCOPY will automatically format the target diskette to the same format as the source diskette, and it will display the following message:

```
Formatting while copying
```

This message indicates that DISKCOPY is formatting the target diskette. When the formatting process is completed, DISKCOPY will make a copy of the source diskette on the target diskette. Unfortunately, the DISKCOPY formatting process does not check for bad sectors. You must format the target diskette using the FORMAT command, before you use DISKCOPY. If a target diskette has bad sectors, you cannot use that disk as the target diskette of the DISKCOPY command. You must also use the CHKDSK command to check for bad sectors on the source diskette. If the source diskette has bad sectors, DISKCOPY will mark the same sectors on the target diskette as bad sectors. If the source diskette contains bad sectors, DISKCOPY will display a message similar to the following when making the copy:

```
Unrecoverable read error on drive A:
Side 0, track 16
Target diskette may be unusable
```

If the source diskette contains bad sectors, you cannot use the DISKCOPY command. With so many disadvantages, you should only use DISKCOPY to copy diskettes that contain hidden files. Diskettes without hidden files should be copied using the COPY *.* command.

DISKCOMP Command

```
Syntax: [D:]DISKCOMP <Source Drive> <Target Drive>
```

The **DISKCOMP command** is a DOS external command used to make certain that the DISKCOPY command made an identical copy on the target disk. If the source and target diskettes are not identical, the DISKCOMP command will display a message indicating the difference. This command would be used if you are using DISKCOPY to make a number of copies of a disk and you want to make sure that every copied disk is identical to the original. DISKCOMP can only be used to compare floppy disks, not hard disks.

COMP Command

```
Syntax: [D:]COMP [D:]filename[.ext]   [D:[filename[.ext]
```

The **COMP (COMPare files) command** is a DOS external command used to compare individual files. It is different from DISKCOMP because only individual files are compared, not entire diskettes. Wildcard characters could be used to compare all identically named files on the two different disks. The COMP command is rarely used.

REN Command

```
Syntax: REN [d:]<Old File Name> <New File Name>
```

The **REN command** is an internal DOS command used to change the file name (either the filename, the extension, or both can be changed) of a file. You may want to change the file name so that it is more descriptive of the file contents. The full name of the command is RENAME but it can be entered as REN. The REN command does not create a new file like the COPY command, it just changes the file name. Because REN does not create a new file, it cannot be used to rename a file stored on one disk to a different disk. If you entered a REN command that specified a target disk drive name DOS will display an error message and will not execute the command. Wildcard characters can be used with the REN command to change the file names of multiple files. The following command will change the file name OLDNAME to a file name of NEWNAME:

```
REN OLDNAME NEWNAME
```

REN Error Messages

Problem: You entered a REN command and DOS displays the following error message:

```
Invalid parameter
```

Solution: This error is displayed when you specify a target disk drive (for example, REN A:OLDNAME B:NEWNAME). The REN command cannot be used to rename a file on one disk to another disk drive. The COPY command could be used to copy a file to another disk drive and assign the copied file a different name.

Problem: You entered a REN command and DOS displays the following error message:

```
Duplicate filename or filename not found
```

Solution: You misspelled the name of the file that you wish to rename or the new file name already exists. Check the spelling of the old file name and take a directory of the disk to see if the new file name exists.

DEL Command

```
Syntax: DEL [d:]filename[.ext]
```

The **DEL (DELete) command** is an internal DOS command used to erase files from a disk. DEL and ERASE are identical commands but DEL will be used because it takes fewer keystrokes. Since the DEL command erases files, you must be very careful with this command. DEL cannot be used to delete hidden files or read-only files. Read-only files are discussed in the section on the ATTRIB command in this chapter. Assuming that the default drive is drive A, the following command would erase a file called OLDFILE from drive A:

```
DEL OLDFILE
```

The DEL command can be used with wildcard characters to selectively delete files. Before you issue a DEL command with wildcards, you should first enter a DIR command with the same wildcards to verify which files will be deleted. For example, if you are going to use the command DEL BUD*, precede this command with the command DIR BUD*, so that you will see a directory of the files that will be deleted. The most powerful and potentially dangerous DEL command is the **DEL *.* command** which tells DOS to erase all files on a disk. If you issue the DEL *.* command, DOS will display the following prompt:

```
ARE YOU SURE (Y/N)?
```

You must press the Y key and then press <ENTER> before DOS will erase the files. FORMAT can also be used to delete all the files on a disk but the FORMAT command will take a over a minute while DEL *.* will take just seconds to delete all the files. DOS Version 4 adds the /P option to the DEL or ERASE commands. If you use the **DEL /P (Pause) option**, DOS will pause and display the name of each file that will be deleted. You can press Y to delete the file or N to leave the file intact.

Enhancing DOS

DOS has no ability to restore deleted files, but several third-party software programs can restore deleted files. When you use the DEL command on a file, DOS does not erase the file from disk, it just causes the file's entry on the disk directory to be flagged as a file that is deleted. The DEL command replaces the first character of the deleted file's filename with ASCII character 229. ASCII (American Standard Code for Information Interchange) is the internal code used by microcomputers to represent each character stored in RAM or on disk. If you use third-party software to undelete a file the first character of the filename will display as a ?. If you accidentally delete a file or files immediately stop working with the disk that contains the file. If you continue to work with that disk, DOS may overwrite the contents of the file with another file because the file has been flagged as a deleted file. You can then use a third-party software package to list the deleted file. You will have to specify which character should replace the ? that DOS entered as the first character of the file. The file will then be undeleted.

ATTRIB Command

```
Syntax: [D:]ATTRIB [+R|-R] [+A|-A] [D:]filename[.ext] [/S]
```

The **ATTRIB command** is a DOS external command used to prevent a file from being accidentally deleted. This command is available only in Version 3.0 or greater. This command can be used to give a file read-only status. A **read-only file** can be read, but cannot be deleted or overwritten. This command is often used at installations that have networked microcomputers together so that users may share the same hard-disk drive. A user can make a file read-only so that other users cannot accidentally erase the file. Wildcards can be used with this command to change the read-only status of a group of files. The **ATTRIB +R parameter** instructs DOS to make a file read-only and the **ATTRIB -R parameter** instructs DOS to remove the read-only status of a file. The **ATTRIB +A parameter** instructs DOS to set the **archive bit** on for a file and the **ATTRIB -A parameter** instructs DOS to set the archive bit off for a file. The use of the archive bit will be covered in chapter eight. The /S option of the ATTRIB command will be covered in chapter six.

92 File Manipulation

You may wish to assign read-only status to important files so that they cannot be accidentally deleted. For example, the DOS system file, COMMAND.COM, must be found on the DOS disk in drive A, or in the root directory of drive C for DOS to be successfully booted. To prevent the file COMMAND.COM from being accidentally deleted the following command would be used:

```
ATTRIB +R COMMAND.COM
```

COMMAND.COM has now become <u>Superfile</u>; it cannot be deleted. If you entered the command: DEL COMMAND.COM, DOS would display the following message:

```
ACCESS DENIED.
```

If an ATTRIB command is entered without any parameters, DOS will display the status of the file. For example, if the default drive is drive A and the command ATTRIB COMMAND.COM is entered, DOS will display the following:

```
A    R    A:\COMMAND.COM
```

The A in the first column indicates the archive bit for the COMMAND.COM file has been turned on. The R denotes that COMMAND.COM is a read-only file. If you want to reverse the process and remove the read-only status of COMMAND.COM, the following command would be used:

```
ATTRIB -R COMMAND.COM
```

Since read-only files cannot be modified or deleted, you should not assign read-only status to data files that will be used by applications programs. When read-only files are copied with COPY or XCOPY, the read-only status is not copied with the file. You must use the ATTRIB command to reassign read-only status to the copied files. Third-party software programs can be used to assign or unassign hidden status to files. DOS has no command to change the hidden status of a file.

ATTRIB Error Message

Problem: You have used a COPY command in which a read-only file has been specified as the target file and DOS displays the following error message:

```
File creation error
```

Solution: The COPY command will not copy to a read-only file. You must use ATTRIB to change the status of the file.

CHKDSK Command

```
Syntax: [D:]CHKDSK [D:][filename[.ext]] [/F] [/V]
```

The **CHKDSK (CHecK DiSK) command** is a DOS external command that displays a disk status report for a specified disk and lists the internal memory status of a microcomputer. The command can also be used to fix errors in the File Allocation Table (FAT). When the command is used, it will display any error messages, followed by a status report. This status report includes the following items:

```
1. The volume label (if any) and the date the disk was
   formatted.
2. The total amount of disk space.
3. The number of files and bytes used by hidden files.
4. The number of files and bytes used by user files.
5. The amount of bytes marked as bad sectors (if any).
6. The number of fragmented files (if any).
7. The amount of free disk space.
8. The amount of RAM installed in the microcomputer.
9. The amount of free RAM available.
```

The most often used statistics on the CHKDSK report are the amount of RAM installed in the microcomputer and the amount of free RAM. Free RAM is the amount of RAM not currently occupied by DOS or applications programs. If an application program refuses to load due to lack of sufficient memory, use the CHKDSK command to display total installed RAM and free RAM. The maximum amount of memory recognized by DOS is 640KB. Your microcomputer may have more than 640KB or RAM installed but only 640KB is recognized by DOS. To find the amount of free disk space, use the DIR command which will display this information much faster than the CHKDSK command. Hidden files are not displayed by the DIR command. If you suspect that a disk contains hidden files, CHKDSK can be used to display the number of files and bytes used by hidden files. The **CHKDSK /V (View) option** can be used to display the filenames of the hidden files. CHKDSK can also be used to display the number of fragmented files. Files are stored on disk in clusters. Files can be erased from disk. As files are erased, the clusters occupied by these files can be used to store other files. If there is not enough room to store a file in consecutive clusters, the file will have to be broken up into one or more fragments, and stored in noncontiguous clusters on the disk. As the number of fragmented files grows, disk access is slowed down. The following command will display the amount of fragmented files on the disk in drive B:

```
A:CHKDSK B:*.*
```

If no fragmented files are found DOS will display the message: ALL SPECIFIED FILE(S) ARE CONTIGUOUS. If fragmented files are found, DOS will display this message for each fragmented file: CONTAINS XXX NONCONTIGUOUS BLOCKS. If the disk checked is a floppy disk, the COPY *.* command can be used to create an unfragmented disk. Use the COPY *.* command to copy all the files from the fragmented disk to an empty disk. The COPY *.* command will copy all files into contiguous clusters, which will speed up the disk access for those files. If the disk checked is a hard disk, DOS has no ability to unfragment a hard disk. Many utility programs, including PC-TOOLS have a program that will unfragment a hard disk. A highly fragmented hard disk will really slow down a microcomputer system.

An error message will be displayed by the CHKDSK command if there are any lost allocation clusters. **Lost allocation clusters** are parts of files that have deleted from the directory, but are still recorded in the File Allocation Table (FAT). This discrepancy will occur because of some malfunction during the file-save process. The errors usually occur when a disk write is in progress and one of the following occurs:

```
1. The user turns off the microcomputer.
2. The user reboots the microcomputer.
3. The user presses <CTRL-BREAK>.
4. A power outage shuts down the microcomputer.
```

If the lost allocation cluster error message is displayed, you can enter the following command to correct the problem (assuming the drive checked is drive B):

```
A:CHKDSK/F B:
```

The **CHKDSK /F (Fix) option** combines any lost clusters on a disk into a series of files named FILEnnn.CHK, where nnn is a consecutive number starting with 001. The /F option should be used periodically to determine if lost allocation clusters exist. Lost allocation clusters indicate a corrupted FAT which may result in a loss of data.

Enhancing DOS

Third-party utility software programs such as Norton Utilities can be used to examine these files and possibly recover all or some of the data. If you cannot recover the data you can then use the DEL command to erase the FILEnnn.CHK files.

CHKDSK /V (View) Option

The CHKDSK /V (View) option is used to list all files in a directory, including hidden files which cannot be displayed with the DIR command. To list all user and hidden files on the disk in drive A use the following command (assuming drive A is the default drive):

```
CHKDSK/V
```

This command will generate a report like the following display:

```
Volume SIDEREAL created Dec 31, 1992   6:50p
Directory A:/
   A:/IO.SYS
   A:/MSDOS.SYS
   A:/SIDEREAL
   A:/COMMAND.COM

 362496 bytes total disk space
  78848 bytes in 3 hidden files
 283648 bytes available on disk

 655360 bytes total memory
 600160 bytes free
```

This disk has been formatted with the [/S] option and has no user files on it. The three hidden files listed include the two DOS hidden system files IO.SYS and MSDOS.SYS (the files would be IBMBIO.COM and IBMDOS.COM on a PC-DOS system) and the volume label file of SIDEREAL.

Terms

Archive bit (91)
ATTRIB (91)
ATTRIB +A parameter (91)
ATTRIB +R parameter (91)
ATTRIB -A parameter (91)
ATTRIB -R parameter (91)
Backup (85)
Backup diskettes (87)
CHKDSK (CHecK DiSK) Command (93)
CHKDSK /F (Fix) option (94)
CHKDSK /V (View) option (93)
COMP (COMPare files) command (89)
COPY command (85)
COPY *.* command (87)
COPY /V (Verify) option (87)
DEL (DELete) command (90)
DEL *.* command (91)
DEL /P {Pause} option (91)
DISKCOMP (89)
DISKCOPY (88)
Lost allocation clusters (94)
Read-only file (91)
REN command (90)
XCOPY command (87)
XCOPY /D (Date) Option (88)
XCOPY /P (Prompt) Option (88)
XCOPY /W (Wait) option (88)

96 File Manipulation

Review Questions

Name _____

Mastery Self-Quiz True/False

Answer T for true or F for false.

1. ___ COPY is used to make copies of existing files.
2. ___ COPY is often used to make backup copies of files.
3. ___ The XCOPY command can be used to selectively copy files by date.
4. ___ XCOPY was introduced in Version 2.0 of DOS.
5. ___ Wildcards cannot be used with the COPY command.
6. ___ DISKCOPY should be used to copy a disk that contains hidden files.
7. ___ If you use DISKCOPY, you should format the target disk first.
8. ___ COPY *.* can be used to unfragment a floppy disk.
9. ___ The REN command creates an additional file.
10. ___ The DEL *.* command requires a Y confirmation.

Mastery Self-Quiz Fill-in

1. The _____ option of the COPY command will make DOS verify the copy.
2. _____ can be used to give a file read-only status.
3. If the target drive name is omitted in a COPY command, DOS will assume the _____ drive.
4. The command _____ will erase a file named FILE1 from drive B.
5. _____ is used to copy the DOS hidden system files to another disk.
6. The _____ option of XCOPY makes DOS prompt the user to confirm each file to be copied.
7. The _____ command changes the name of a file.
8. _____ will delete all the files on a disk.
9. The _____ command is used to compare two diskettes.
10. _____ is used to compare two files to see if they are identical.

Discussion Questions

1. What are some of the shortcuts that can be used with the COPY command?

2. DISKCOPY and COPY *.* are similar commands. When is it appropriate to use these commands?

3. What unique information is displayed by the CHKDSK command?

Chapter Five 97

Solving Error Messages

Enter the solution to each of these problems.

Problem: You entered a COPY command and DOS displays the following error message:

```
File cannot be copied onto itself
    0 File(s) copied
```

Solution:

Problem: You entered a COPY command and DOS displays the following error message:

```
Insufficient disk space, 0 file(s) copied.
```

Solution:

Problem: You entered a COPY command in which a read-only file has been specified as the target file and DOS displays the following error message:

```
File creation error
```

Solution:

Problem: You entered a REN command and DOS displays the following error message:

```
Invalid parameter
```

Solution:

Problem: You entered a REN command and DOS displays the following error message:

```
Duplicate filename or filename not found
```

Solution:

Chapter Five Tutorial

If you are using a floppy-disk system, you will follow the steps labeled floppy-disk users. If you are using a hard-disk system, you will follow the steps labeled hard-disk users. If you are using a hard-disk system turn to page 102, otherwise do the instructions that follow.

Floppy-Disk Users

Startup

1. Insert the DOS system disk in drive A and insert the data disk (your disk) in drive B.
2. Do a warm boot and enter the date and time.
3. TYPE: **PATH A:** <ENTER>
4. TYPE: **PROMPT PG** <ENTER>
   [DOS will display the following prompt:]

```
A:\>
```

COPY Command

The COPY command is used to make duplicates of existing files on the same disk or on another disk. The first file (or file pattern if wildcards are used) is called the source file and the second file is called the target file.]

1. TYPE: **COPY A:DISKCOPY.COM B:DISKCOPY.COM** <ENTER>
   [A:DISKCOPY.COM is the source file and B:DISKCOPY.COM is the target file. DOS should respond with: "1 File(s) copied", showing that your copy operation worked.]
2. TYPE: **DIR/W B:** <ENTER>
   [Your screen should match the following display of files:]

```
DISKCOPY     COM
```

COPY Command Shortcuts

1. TYPE: **COPY DISKCOPY.COM B:** <ENTER>
   [The source file is copied from the default drive (drive A, since you started this operation with the A:\> prompt) to the target drive. It is copied with the same name since you did not supply a different name. DOS should respond with: "1 File(s) copied", showing that the copy operation worked.]
2. TYPE: **CLS** <ENTER>

Copy a File and Change Its Name

1. TYPE: **COPY DISKCOPY.COM B:NEWFILE** <ENTER>
   [The source file, DISKCOPY.COM, is copied to the target drive with a different name. DOS should respond with: "1 File(s) copied", showing that the copy operation worked.]
2. TYPE: **DIR/W B:** <ENTER>
   [Your display of files should match the following:]

```
DISKCOPY    COM     NEWFILE
```

3. TYPE: **CLS** <ENTER>

COPY Command With Wildcards

1. TYPE: **COPY DISKCO??.COM B:** <ENTER>
   [DOS responds with the following display showing that two files were copied (DISKCOPY and DISKCOMP). The display shows that both files were copied with a single copy command. The COPY command accepted the PY in DISKCOPY and the MP in DISKCOMP because of the ?? wildcards in the source file parameter.]

```
DISKCOMP.COM
DISKCOPY.COM
    2 File(s) copied
```

2. TYPE: **DIR/W B:** <ENTER>
   [Your display of files should match the following:]

```
DISKCOPY    COM     NEWFILE     DISKCOMP    COM
```

3. TYPE: **COPY D*.* B:** <ENTER>
   [DOS will copy all files that begin with D and have any extension. DOS will respond with the following display that shows that it copied every file that began with a D:]

```
DISKCOMP.COM
DISKCOPY.COM
DISPLAY.SYS
DRIVER.SYS
    4 File(s) copied
```

4. TYPE: **CLS** <ENTER>

100 File Manipulation

Copying a file on the Same Disk

1. TYPE: **B:** <ENTER>
   [Your screen should match the following:]

```
B:\>
```

2. **If you do not have this prompt check with computer center personnel.**
3. TYPE: **DIR/W** <ENTER>
   [Your display of files should match the following:]

```
DISKCOPY COM   NEWFILE   DISKCOMP COM   DISPLAY   SYS   DRIVER.SYS
```

4. TYPE: **COPY DRIVER.SYS D.SYS** <ENTER>
   [You have copied a file on the same disk and changed the name of that file.]
5. TYPE: **DIR/W** <ENTER>
   [Note that you still have the original file (DRIVER.SYS) and the copied file (D.SYS) on the disk. Your display of files should match the following:]

```
DISKCOPY COM   NEWFILE   DISKCOMP COM   DISPLAY   SYS   DRIVER SYS
D        SYS
```

REN Command

The REN command is used to change the name of a file. This command does not create a new file like the COPY command; the REN command just changes the name of a file.

1. TYPE: **REN DISKCOPY.COM NEWNAME** <ENTER>
   [You have changed the name of the file DISKCOPY.COM to NEWNAME.]
2. TYPE: **DIR/W** <ENTER>
   [Your display of files should match the following:]

```
NEWNAME        NEWFILE   DISKCOMP   COM   DISPLAY   SYS   DRIVER.SYS
D        SYS
```

3. TYPE: **CLS** <ENTER>

Using the DEL Command to Delete a Single File

The DEL command is used to erase files. You will use a DEL command to erase a single file.

1.   TYPE: **DEL NEWNAME** <ENTER>
   [This command will delete the file NEWNAME.]
2.   TYPE: **DIR/W** <ENTER>
   [Note that the file NEWNAME is no longer listed because it has been deleted. Your screen should match the following:]

```
NEWFILE        DISKCOMP COM    DISPLAY  SYS    DRIVER  SYS    D       SYS
```

*Using the DEL *.* Command*

The DEL command is used to erase files on a disk. The DEL *.* will erase every file in the current directory. Since this is a powerful command, DOS will make you confirm the command by responding Y to the prompt: ARE YOU SURE (Y/N)?

1.   **Make sure that you have the B:\ > prompt.**
2.   TYPE: **DEL *.*** <ENTER>
   [DOS will display the following prompt:]

```
ARE YOU SURE (Y/N)?
```

3.   This prompt is warning you that you are going to delete every file on the diskette.
4.   PRESS: **Y** <ENTER>
   [You have deleted every file on the disk in drive B.]
5.   TYPE: **CLS** <ENTER>
6.   TYPE: **DIR/W** <ENTER>
   [DOS should display the screen shown below, proving that all files have been deleted from drive B.]

```
Volume in drive B is {Your last name}
Directory of B:\

File not found
```

7.   You have completed tutorial five. You can go back to the beginning of the floppy-disk users section on page 98 and do it again, or you can do comprehensive problem five on page 105.

102 File Manipulation

Hard-Disk Users

Startup

1. Do a warm boot.
2. Insert your data disk in drive A.
3. TYPE: **PROMPT PG** <ENTER>
4. TYPE: **PATH C:\;C:\DT** <ENTER>
5. TYPE: **CD\DT** <ENTER>
   [DOS should display the following prompt:]

```
C:\DT>
```

6. If your prompt does not match the C:\DT> prompt, check with your instructor or computer center personnel and do not do any more steps until you have the C:\DT> prompt.

COPY Command

The COPY command is used to make duplicates of existing files on the same disk or on another disk. The first file (or file pattern if wildcards are used) is called the source file and the second file is called the target file.]

1. TYPE: **COPY C:\DT\DISKCOPY.COM A:DISKCOPY.COM** <ENTER>
   [C:\DT\DISKCOPY.COM is the source file and A:DISKCOPY.COM is the target file. DOS should respond with: "1 File(s) copied", showing that your copy operation worked.]
2. TYPE: **DIR/W A:** <ENTER>
   [Your screen should match the following display of files:]

```
DISKCOPY     COM
```

COPY Command Shortcuts

1. TYPE: **COPY DISKCOPY.COM A:** <ENTER>
   [The source file is copied from the default drive (drive C, since you started this operation with the C:\DT> prompt) to the target drive. It is copied with the same name since you did not supply a different name. DOS should respond with: "1 File(s) copied", showing that the copy operation worked.]
2. TYPE: **CLS** <ENTER>

Copy a File and Change Its Name

1. TYPE: **COPY DISKCOPY.COM A:NEWFILE** <ENTER>
   [The source file, DISKCOPY.COM, is copied to the target drive with a different name. DOS should respond with: "1 File(s) copied", showing that the copy operation worked.]
2. TYPE: **DIR/W A:** <ENTER>
   [Your display of files should match the following:]

```
DISKCOPY     COM       NEWFILE
```

COPY Command With Wildcards

1. TYPE: **COPY DISKCO??.COM A:** <ENTER>
   [DOS responds with the following display showing that two files were copied (DISKCOPY and DISK-COMP). The display shows that both files were copied with a single copy command. The COPY command accepted the PY in DISKCOPY and the MP in DISKCOMP because of the ?? wildcards in the source file parameter.]

```
DISKCOMP.COM
DISKCOPY.COM
    2 File(s) copied
```

2. TYPE: **DIR/W A:** <ENTER>
   [Your display of files should match the following:]

```
DISKCOPY   COM    NEWFILE    DISKCOMP   COM
```

3. TYPE: **COPY D*.* A:** <ENTER>
   [DOS will copy all files that begin with D and have any extension. DOS will respond with the following display that shows that it copied every file that began with a D:]

```
DISKCOMP.COM
DISKCOPY.COM
DISPLAY.SYS
DRIVER.SYS
    4 File(s) copied
```

4. TYPE: **CLS** <ENTER>

Copying a file on the Same Disk

1. TYPE: **A:** <ENTER>
   [Your screen should match the following:]

```
A:\>
```

2. **If you do not have this prompt check with computer center personnel.**

104 File Manipulation

3.   TYPE: **DIR/W** <ENTER>
       [Your display of files should match the following:]

```
DISKCOPY   COM      NEWFILE    DISKCOMP  COM     DISPLAY  SYS    DRIVER SYS
```

4.   TYPE: **COPY DRIVER.SYS D.SYS** <ENTER>
       [You have copied a file on the same disk and changed the name of that file.]
5.   TYPE: **DIR/W** <ENTER>
       [Note that you still have the original file (DRIVER.SYS) and the copied file (D.SYS) on the disk. Your display of files should match the following:]

```
DISKCOPY   COM      NEWFILE    DISKCOMP  COM     DISPLAY  SYS    DRIVER SYS
D          SYS
```

REN Command

The REN command is used to change the name of a file. This command does not create a new file like the COPY command, the REN command just changes the name of a file.

1.   TYPE: **REN DISKCOPY.COM NEWNAME** <ENTER>
       [You have changed the name of the file DISKCOPY.COM to NEWNAME.]
2.   TYPE: **DIR/W** <ENTER>
       [Your display of files should match the following:]

```
NEWNAME             NEWFILE    DISKCOMP  COM     DISPLAY  SYS    DRIVER SYS
D          SYS
```

3.   TYPE: **CLS** <ENTER>

Using the DEL Command to Delete a Single File

The DEL command is used to erase files. You will use a DEL command to erase a single file.

1.   TYPE: **DEL NEWNAME** <ENTER>
       [This command will delete the file NEWNAME.]
2.   TYPE: **DIR/W** <ENTER>
       [Note that the file NEWNAME is no longer listed because it has been deleted. Your screen should match the following:]

```
NEWFILE    DISKCOMP  COM     DISPLAY  SYS    DRIVER    SYS    D    SYS
```

Using the DEL *.* Command

The DEL command is used to erase files on a disk. The DEL *.* will erase every file in the current directory. Since this is a powerful command, DOS will make you confirm the command by responding Y to the prompt: ARE YOU SURE (Y/N)?

1. **Make sure that you have the A:\> prompt.**
2. TYPE: **DEL *.*** <ENTER>
   [DOS will display the following prompt:]

```
ARE YOU SURE (Y/N)?
```

3. This prompt is warning you that you are going to delete every file on the diskette.
4. PRESS: **Y** <ENTER>
   [You have deleted every file on the disk in drive A.]
5. TYPE: **CLS** <ENTER>
6. TYPE: **DIR/W** <ENTER>
   [DOS should display the screen shown below, proving that all files have been deleted from drive B.]

```
Volume in drive A is {Your last name}
Directory of A:\

File not found
```

7. You have completed tutorial five. You can go back to the beginning of the hard-disk users section on page 102 and do it again, or you can do comprehensive problem five.

Comprehensive Problem Five

Floppy-Disk Users

1. Change to drive B and make sure that you have the B:\> prompt. If there are any files on your disk (the disk in drive B) delete them all.
2. If you do not have a label on your disk, use the LABEL command to put a label of the first eleven characters of your last name on the disk.
3. Change to drive A and make sure you have the A:\> prompt.
4. Copy all files on drive A that have a filename beginning with D and any extension to drive B.
5. Take a wide directory of drive B. Your display of files should match the following.

```
DISKCOMP COM    DISKCOPY COM    DISPLAY  SYS    DRIVER  SYS
```

6. Copy all files on drive A that have an extension of .EXE to drive B.
7. Take a wide directory of drive B. Your display of files should match the following:

106 File Manipulation

```
DISKCOMP COM DISKCOPY COM DISPLAY  SYS DRIVER SYS APPEND EXE
ATTRIB   EXE EXE2BIN  EXE FASTOPEN EXE FIND   EXE JOIN   EXE
NLSFUNC  EXE SORT     EXE SUBST    EXE
```

Deleting and Renaming Files

1. Change to drive B. Make sure that your prompt is B:\>.
2. Delete all files on drive B that have an extension of .SYS.
3. Take a wide directory of drive B. Your display of files should match the following:

```
DISKCOMP COM DISKCOPY COM APPEND EXE ATTRIB  EXE EXE2BIN EXE
FASTOPEN EXE FIND     EXE JOIN   EXE NLSFUNC EXE SORT    EXE
SUBST    EXE
```

4. Rename all files on drive B that have filenames beginning with with DISK so that their filenames begin with DUCK.
5. Take a wide directory of drive B. Your display of files should match the following:

```
DUCKCOMP COM DUCKCOPY COM APPEND EXE ATTRIB  EXE EXE2BIN EXE
FASTOPEN EXE FIND     EXE JOIN   EXE NLSFUNC EXE SORT    EXE
SUBST    EXE
```

6. If your display matches, use the redirection operator to print a wide directory of drive B. Turn in this printout.

Hard-Disk Users

1. Change to drive A and make sure that you have the A:\> prompt. If there are any files on your disk (the disk in drive A) delete them all.
2. If you do not have a label on your disk, use the LABEL command to put a label of the first eleven characters of your last name on the disk.
3. Change to drive C and make sure you have the C:\DT> prompt.
4. Copy all files on drive C that have a filename beginning with D and any extension to drive A.
5. Take a wide directory of drive A. Your display of files should match the following:

```
DISKCOMP COM    DISKCOPY COM    DISPLAY  SYS    DRIVER  SYS
```

6. Copy all files on drive C that have an extension of .EXE to drive A.
7. Take a wide directory of drive A. Your display of files should match the following:

```
DISKCOMP COM DISKCOPY COM DISPLAY  SYS DRIVER SYS APPEND EXE
ATTRIB   EXE EXE2BIN  EXE FASTOPEN EXE FIND   EXE JOIN   EXE
NLSFUNC  EXE SORT     EXE SUBST    EXE
```

Deleting and Renaming Files

1. Change to drive A. Make sure that your prompt is A:\>.
2. Delete all files on drive A that have an extension of .SYS.
3. Take a wide directory of drive A. Your display of files should match the following:

```
DISKCOMP COM DISKCOPY COM APPEND EXE ATTRIB  EXE EXE2BIN EXE
FASTOPEN EXE FIND     EXE JOIN   EXE NLSFUNC EXE SORT    EXE
SUBST    EXE
```

4. Rename all files on drive A that have a filename beginining with DISK so that their filenames begin with DUCK.
5. Take a wide directory of drive A. Your display of files should match the following:

```
DUCKCOMP COM DUCKCOPY COM APPEND EXE ATTRIB  EXE EXE2BIN EXE
FASTOPEN EXE FIND     EXE JOIN   EXE NLSFUNC EXE SORT    EXE
SUBST    EXE
```

6. If your display matches, use the redirection operator to print a wide directory of drive A. Turn in this printout.

Subdirectory System

Chapter 6

Learning Objectives

After completing chapter six the student will be able to:

```
1. Define the purpose of a subdirectory system.
2. Use the MD command to create subdirectories.
3. Use the CD command to change the current subdirectory.
4. Use the RD command to erase a subdirectory.
5. Use the COPY command to copy files to subdirectories.
6. Use the XCOPY command to copy a subdirectory system.
7. Use the TREE command to display the subdirectory system.
```

Root Directory

Every disk has a directory called the root directory or upper-level directory which is created by DOS when the disk is formatted. This initial directory is called the root directory because the subdirectories (directories created by the user) grow from the root. The root directory, a reserved section of the disk, is used to store files and subdirectory files. The root directory of a hard disk should only contain a few files: the DOS system files (the two hidden files and COMMAND.COM), the CONFIG.SYS file, the AUTOEXEC.BAT file, and other batch files created by the user (batch files are discussed in chapter seven). The root directory will also contain the names of one or more subdirectories which are directories created by the user.

Subdirectory System

Hard disks have storage space to store thousands of files. If all of the files were contained within a single directory, DOS would operate slowly and it would be difficult to locate a file. A series of subdirectories forming a **subdirectory system** must be created by the user to organize a hard disk. Imagine a file cabinet purchased to store your paper files. It would be foolish to stuff every piece of paper into one file folder. An efficient filing system would have a separate file folder for each group of related information. Subdirectories organize a disk in exactly the same way. You can create a separate file folder (subdirectory) for each group of related information. You can have a separate subdirectory for word processing files, spreadsheet files, and database files. The data files for each program should be in a separate subdirectory from the program files. For example, the LOTUS 1-2-3 program should be in one subdirectory and data files created by that program should be in a separate subdirectory. When you back up the hard disk, you will only have to back up the program directory once but the data directory must be backed repeatedly. When you get a new version of a program, it will be more easily installed if the program files are separated from the data files. A subdirectory system is required to organized the data stored on a hard drive. Floppy diskettes (especially high-density floppies) can also be organized into a series of subdirectories. In addition to organizing a disk, creating subdirectories solves a physical storage problem. Diskettes can only contain from 112 to 224 files in the root directory, depending upon the storage capacity of the diskette, and a hard disk can only contain 512 files in the root directory, but a subdirectory can contain an unlimited amount of files.

Subdirectories

The terms directory and subdirectory are used interchangeably, but technically only the root directory is a directory; all other directories are subdirectories. A subdirectory is a special type of file that contains the names of all the files that are placed within that subdirectory and it may also contain the names of other subdirectories that are subsidiary to it. A directory (either the root directory created by DOS or a subdirectory created by the user) that has one or more subdirectories created underneath it is known as a **parent directory**. Since a subdirectory is a file to DOS, the same DOS file name rules apply to subdirectory names. You should not use an extension as part of the name of a subdirectory. You cannot assign a name to a subdirectory that is the same as a file name in the parent directory.

Subdirectories and Files

If you use the DIR command without the /P or /W options, DOS displays the designation <DIR> next to a subdirectory file in the directory display. The default drive is drive B. WP is the only subdirectory created on a disk in drive B. A file called X is also stored in the root directory. If you issued the DIR command, DOS would display the following:

```
DIRECTORY OF B:\
WP          <DIR>  12-31-92       8:00A
X           2000   10-16-92      11:00A
```

The display DIRECTORY OF B:\ identifies the drive and the directory that was displayed. The backslash character (\) is used by DOS to represent the root directory. The backslash character is called the **path symbol** because it is used to steer DOS to the correct subdirectory. Since the backslash is a one of the special characters used by DOS as delimiter, you do not have to leave a space before the backslash. If you do not assign extensions to your subdirectory names the following command will display all the subdirectories names in a particular subdirectory:

```
DIR *.
```

Current Directory

When you boot DOS, the default drive will always be the drive from which you booted DOS (drive A on a floppy system and drive C on a hard-disk system), and the **current directory** or **default directory** will always be the root directory. Just as you can change drives, you can also change directories. The directory that you change to becomes the current directory. If you have more than one drive, each drive can have a current directory. As you switch between drives, DOS will position you in the current directory for each drive.

Directory Path

When you issue a DOS command, DOS will apply that command to the default drive if you do not provide a target drive as part of the command. When you issue a DOS command, DOS will apply that command to the current directory of the default drive if you do not provide a target directory as part of the command. If you want a command to apply to a directory other than the current directory you must supply DOS with the full **pathname** of a subdirectory that you want the command to apply to. A pathname begins with the path symbol (\) indicating that DOS will start searching from the root directory. The initial path symbol (\) is followed by a series of subdirectory names separated by the path symbol (\). Assume that the current directory is B:\ (the root directory of drive B). The following DIR command would display a listing of the WP subdirectory:

```
DIR\WP
```

If you just entered DIR, DOS would have displayed a directory of B:\ (the current directory). The backslash in the command DIR\WP tells DOS to look in the root directory for a subdirectory called WP. The listing generated by the DIR\WP command would be as follows:

```
DIRECTORY OF B:\WP
.         <DIR>         12-31-92         8:00A
..        <DIR>         12-31-92         8:00A
```

Each new subdirectory is created with two files, the directory entry file (.) and the parent directory file (..). The parent directory file (..) is used to point to the parent directory (the directory above the current directory). The directory entry file (.) is used to point to the current directory (the WP subdirectory in this case). The directory entry file name (.) can be used to shorten commands. For example, if you wanted to copy every file in a directory to drive B you could enter either COPY . B: or COPY *.* B:. Since the period (.) stands for the current directory, the command COPY . B: would instruct DOS to copy every file in the current directory to drive B.

Full Pathname

If a command that you enter is to apply to a drive other than the default drive, the target drive name must also be included in the full pathname. For example, the default drive is B, and you want to list the directory of the \XYZ subdirectory on drive C. The full pathname C:\XYZ must be used to direct DOS to drive C and the \XYZ directory. If you did not provide the disk drive, DOS would look for an \XYZ directory on drive B.

Subdirectories within Subdirectories

You can create subdirectories underneath subdirectories. For example, a subdirectory called \WP\OLDLTR could be created underneath the \WP subdirectory to file away old letters. To display a listing of the \WP\OLDLTR subdirectory, DOS must be provided with a full pathname. Assuming that \WP\OLDLTR is located on the default drive the following command would display a directory of the \WP\OLDLTR subdirectory:

```
DIR\WP\OLDLTR
```

The first backslash directs DOS to search the root directory for a subdirectory called \WP. The second backslash directs DOS to search the subdirectory \WP for a subdirectory called \WP\OLDLTR. You can have an unlimited number of subdirectories and you can have many levels of subdirectories underneath your subdirectories. For example, you could create another subdirectory underneath \WP\OLDLTR called \WP\OLDLTR\OLDERLTR. As you can see, if you create more than two levels of subdirectories your filing system becomes very complex. Design your subdirectory system so that you create only two levels of subdirectories.

Subdirectory Commands

MD Command

```
Syntax: MD [D:][PATH]<SUBDIRECTORY NAME>
```

The **MD {Make Directory} command** is a DOS internal command used to create subdirectories. The full name of the command is MKDIR but it can be abbreviated as MD. The only parameter that you must specify is the subdirectory name. If you omit the drive parameter, DOS will use the default drive. If you omit the path parameter, DOS will create the subdirectory underneath the current directory on the default drive. For example, the default drive and directory is B:\ when you issue the following command:

```
MD\WP
```

Since you did not specify a drive, DOS assumed drive B, and since you specified a path of \WP, DOS would create the subdirectory underneath the root directory. The following command would create a subdirectory called \WP\OLDLTR underneath the WP subdirectory:

```
MD\WP\OLDLTR
```

MD Error Message

Problem: You entered the MD command and DOS displays the following message:

```
Unable to create directory
```

Solution: The directory already exists or you are trying to create a directory that has the same filename as a file in the root directory. Check to see if the directory exists and, if necessary, use another name.

CD Command

```
Syntax: CD [D:][PATH]
```

The CD {Change Directory} command is a DOS internal command used to change the current subdirectory on a particular drive. The full name of the command is CHDIR but it can be abbreviated as CD. When you boot DOS, the default drive will always be the drive from which you booted DOS (drive A on a floppy system and drive C on a hard-disk system), and the current directory will always be the root directory of the boot drive (either A:\ or C:\). If you change the current directory, it will simplify your DOS commands because you will not have to provide DOS with a path. For example, if you wished to work with some of the files in the \WP subdirectory (which is on the default drive) you would have to provide DOS with a path of \WP for all of your commands. The following command will change the current subdirectory to the WP subdirectory:

```
CD\WP
```

This command will change the current subdirectory to the \WP\OLDLTR subdirectory:

```
CD\WP\OLDLTR
```

These commands will change the current subdirectory back to the WP subdirectory:

```
CD\WP
or
CD..
```

Since the (..) file is the parent directory file, the **CD.. command** moves up one directory level to the parent directory of the current directory (from \WP\OLDLTR to \WP). The following command will change the current directory to the root directory:

```
CD\
```

The **CD\ command** will always return you to the root directory. No matter how many levels deep you are in the subdirectory structure, CD\ will change the current directory to the root directory. The CD command has several possible parameters:

COMMAND	DOS ACTION
CD.. CD\ CD\WP	DOS moves up one directory level. DOS changes to the root directory. DOS changes to the subdirectory entered.

CD commands

If the directory that you are changing to is not on the default drive, you must first enter the command to change drives and then enter the command to change directories. For example, if the default drive is C and you wish to change to the \WP directory on drive B, you would have to enter the following commands:

```
B:
CD\WP
```

The command CD B:\WP, would make \WP the current directory on drive B but would not make B the default drive.

CD Error Message

Problem: You entered a CD command and DOS displayed the following error message:

```
Invalid Directory
```

Solution: You misspelled the directory name or omitted one or more path symbols.

RD Command

```
Syntax: RD [D:]<PATH>
```

The **RD {Remove Directory} command** is a DOS internal command used to erase a subdirectory. The full name of the command is RMDIR but it can be abbreviated as RD. Even though DOS treats a subdirectory as a file, you must use the RD command instead of the DEL command to erase a subdirectory. DOS makes it difficult to accidentally erase a subdirectory because a subdirectory may contain hundreds of files. You can only remove a subdirectory that contains just the (.) and the (..) files. This means that the subdirectory that you wish to remove must first be purged of any other files and/or subdirectories. You cannot remove the current subdirectory. This rule means that you must change to some other subdirectory before using the RD command. You cannot erase the root directory. For example, if you wished to remove the \WP\OLDLTR subdirectory, you would first have to use the DEL command to remove all files from the \WP\OLDLTR subdirectory. You would then have to move out of the \WP\OLDLTR subdirectory and then issue the following command:

```
RD\WP\OLDLTR
```

The subdirectory \WP\OLDLTR has now been placed in the subdirectory burial ground. You cannot issue the command as simply RD. Since DOS won't remove the current subdirectory, you must provide a path parameter.

RD Error Message

Problem: You entered a RD command and DOS displays the following error message:

```
Invalid path, not directory,
or directory not empty
```

Solution: RD will only remove a directory that is empty. You must purge the directory of all files and/or subdirectories before you can remove it. If the directory is empty, you must change to some other directory. RD will not remove the current directory.

Path Command

When you boot DOS, the default search path is set to the current directory. This means that DOS will only search the current directory for an external DOS command. The PATH command extends the search path that DOS uses to find DOS external commands (or other programs with extensions of COM, EXE, or BAT). The DOS external commands will be on the root directory of drive A on a floppy-disk system, or in a subdirectory (usually C:\DOS) on the hard disk. The PATH command is optional on a floppy-disk system because you could preface all DOS external commands with a drive parameter of A:. The PATH command is an absolute necessity on a hard disk because a hard disk may contain many subdirectories, and only one of those subdirectories will contain the DOS external commands. For example, your system may have DOS stored in the C:\DOS subdirectory. If you issued a path command of PATH C:\DOS, you could then issue any DOS external command from any subdirectory on your hard disk. If DOS could not find the command in the current directory, DOS would then search the C:\DOS subdirectory for the command. If you did not set a search path of C:\DOS, you would have to preface each DOS command with C:\DOS. The semicolon may be used to specify multiple search paths. For example, if you wanted DOS to search both the root directory of drive C and the DOS subdirectory, you could issue the following command:

```
PATH C:\;C:\DOS
```

Issuing a PATH command does not change the current directory. After a search path is set with the PATH command, the search path remains set until you reboot. You can only have one search path active at a time (entering a new path command cancels the old one). Typing the PATH command with no parameters displays the current path. You can cancel all search paths by issuing this command:

```
PATH ;
```

DOS follows a particular sequence when it searches for commands. Within each subdirectory, DOS looks for a matching command with a .COM extension first. If it does not find one, it searches for a matching command with an .EXE extension, and finally a .BAT extension. The PATH command directs DOS to search only for commands (files with extensions of .EXE, .COM, and .BAT), not data files. For example, you have set a search path of A:\ and the current directory is B:\. You wish to erase a file that is named X, and X is found in the root directory on drive A. If you issue the command DEL X, DOS will issue the error message FILE NOT FOUND, because this file is found on drive A. DOS will search for commands, not files. You must change the command to DEL A:X.

Copying Files to Subdirectories

The COPY command will only copy files in the current directory unless you specify the full path for the COPY command. For example, you have created a subdirectory called \WP and a subdirectory called \WP\OLDLTR. Both of these subdirectories are on the default drive. The current directory is the root directory. You wish to copy a file called X from the root directory to the \WP subdirectory. The COPY command would be entered as follows:

```
COPY X \WP
```

You must precede WP with the path character (\) to tell DOS that it should move from the root directory down to the WP subdirectory. If you wanted to change the name of the copied file to Y, you would have to issue the following command:

```
COPY X \WP\Y
```

The path character (\) is used to separate subdirectories from the root directory and also to separate subdirectories from file names. The first backslash directs DOS to move one step below the root directory, and the second backslash tells DOS to assign the copied file a file name of Y in the \WP subdirectory. If you wanted to copy the file X from the root directory to the \WP\OLDLTR subdirectory, and you wanted to change the file name to Y, you would issue the following command:

```
COPY X \WP\OLDLTR\Y
```

You cannot have two files with the same file name in the root directory of a disk. You could, however, have two files with the same name on a disk as long as the files are in different subdirectories. DOS can differentiate between \WP\X and \WP\OLDLTR\X because the pathnames are different. If you want to copy a file from one subdirectory to another subdirectory, the command will be simplified if you use the CD command to make one of the subdirectories the current directory. For example, you want to copy the file XYZ from the \WP\OLDLTR subdirectory to the \WP subdirectory and copy the file with the same file name. If you issued the COPY command with the root directory as the current directory, the command would have to be entered as the following:

```
COPY    \WP\OLDLTR\XYZ  \WP
```

116 Subdirectory System

If you use the CD command to make \WP\OLDLTR the current directory, the command would be simplified to the following:

```
COPY XYZ    \WP
```

Making the \WP\OLDLTR the current directory means that you do not have to provide DOS with a pathname to that subdirectory.

XCOPY /S and /E Options

The XCOPY command was introduced in chapter five and the /W, /P, and /D options were covered in that chapter. The /S and /E options will be covered in this chapter. The XCOPY command, introduced in Version 3.2, can be used to copy the subdirectory structure of one disk to another disk. You have created a subdirectory structure on drive C that has a subdirectory called \WP and two subdirectories called \WP\CUR and \WP\OLD that were created underneath \WP. You want to copy this subdirectory structure to a disk in drive A. Without using the XCOPY command, you would have to create the subdirectory structure on drive A, and then use three separate copy commands to copy files to the three subdirectories. The following XCOPY command can be used to copy the complete subdirectory structure to a disk in drive A:

```
XCOPY C:\WP\*.* A:\ /S/E
```

The COPY command would just copy the contents of the \WP subdirectory to the current directory of drive A. The XCOPY command with the **XCOPY /S (Subdirectory) option** will create the \WP, \WP\CUR, and \WP\OLD subdirectories on drive A and copy the files in those subdirectories from drive C to drive A. If the subdirectories already exist on drive A, XCOPY will just copy the files in the subdirectories from drive C to drive A. The **XCOPY /E (Empty directory) option** directs the XCOPY command to create directories on the target drive even if the directories are empty on the source drive. Without the /E option, empty directories on the source drive would not be created on the target drive.

TREE Command

```
Syntax: [D:]TREE [D:] [/F]
```

As you increase the number of subdirectories on a disk, it will become difficult to remember the names of all of them. The DOS external command **TREE** displays all the subdirectory paths on the default drive. The TREE > PRN command is used to print the subdirectory structure of the disk. If you issue the command with the **TREE /F (File) option**, DOS will also display all the files in the root directory and in each subdirectory. The CHKDSK/V command will list all the files on a disk with their complete pathnames while TREE/F will just list the filenames. The CHKDSK command without the /V option will list the number of directories on the disk and the space occupied by the directory entries. A disk has two subdirectories called WP and LOTUS created on it. The WP directory has a subdirectory called \WP\OLDLTR. If a TREE command was entered, the following directory path listing would be displayed:

```
DIRECTORY PATH LISTING FOR VOLUME ??????????

PATH:\WP

SUB-DIRECTORIES:      OLDLTR

PATH: \WP\OLDLTR

SUB-DIRECTORIES:      NONE

PATH:LOTUS

SUB-DIRECTORIES:      NONE
```

The DOS Version 4 TREE command uses line-drawing characters to draw a visual tree structure of the disk. Version 4 also provides the **TREE /A (ASCII) option** which can be used if your printer will not print the visual tree. The /A option substitutes normal keyboard characters for the default characters and allows the tree display to be printed on any printer.

Enhancing DOS

Commercial software programs like XTREE and PC-TOOLS provide an visual tree structure on the screen which makes navigating the tree structure of a disk much easier than using DOS. Both of these software programs can be used to rename directories, a task impossible with DOS.

ATTRIB /S Option

The **ATTRIB /S (Subdirectory) option** was introduced in Version 3.3 of DOS. If this optional switch is used, it instructs DOS to also process files that match the filespec used in all subdirectories of the directory specified in the command. For example, the following command will assign read-only status to the file XYZ in the \WP directory and will also assign read-only status to any files named XYZ that are found in subdirectories of the \WP directory:

```
ATTRIB/S \WP\XYZ
```

Terms

ATTRIB /S (Subdirectory) option (117)
CD.. command, (112)
CD\ command (112)
Current directory (109)
MD {Make Directory} command (111)
Parent directory (109)
Path symbol (109)
Pathname (110)
RD {Remove Directory} command (113)
Subdirectory system (108)
TREE (116)
TREE /A (ASCII) option (117)
TREE /F (File) option (116)
XCOPY /E (Empty directory) option (116)
XCOPY /S (Subdirectory) option (116)

Review Questions

Name _____

Mastery Self-Quiz True/False

Answer T for true or F for false.

1. ___ Subdirectories are optional on a hard disk system.
2. ___ The top directory is called the root directory.
3. ___ A parent directory is the subdirectory above the current subdirectory.
4. ___ Subdirectories are created with the MD command.
5. ___ The command DIR\WP will display the files in the root directory.
6. ___ The command CD.. will move you up one subdirectory level.
7. ___ The command CD\ will move you up to the root directory.
8. ___ The ATTRIB/S option is used to change the read-only status of files in subdirectories.
9. ___ You can remove a subdirectory by using the DEL *.* command.
10. ___ The RD command can be used to remove the current directory.

Mastery Self-Quiz Fill-in

1. The _____ command is used to change subdirectories.
2. The _____ command moves you up to the root directory.
3. The _____ command moves you up one subdirectory level.
4. The _____ command is used to create a subdirectory.
5. The _____ command is used to remove a subdirectory.
6. The _____ command displays the subdirectories on a disk.
7. The _____ command displays the subdirectories on a disk and the files in each subdirectory.
8. The _____ command will list all files on the disk with their complete pathnames.
9. The _____ command will display the current path.
10. The _____ command cancels all search paths.

Discussion Questions

1. Why are subdirectories necessary?

2. What are the steps involved in removing a subdirectory?

3. Explain the use of the XCOPY /S and /E options.

120 Subdirectory System

Solving Error Messages

Enter the solution to each of these problems.

Problem: You entered the MD command and DOS displays the following error message:

```
Unable to create directory
```

Solution:

Problem: You entered a CD command and DOS displayed the following error message:

```
Invalid Directory
```

Solution:

Problem: You entered a RD command and DOS displays the following error message:

```
Invalid path, not directory,
or directory not empty
```

Solution:

Chapter Six Tutorial

If you are using a floppy-disk system, you will follow the steps labeled floppy-disk users. If you are using a hard-disk system, you will follow the steps labeled hard-disk users. If you are using a hard-disk system turn to page 126, otherwise do the instructions that follow.

Floppy-Disk Users

Startup

1. Insert the DOS system disk in drive A and insert the data disk (your disk) in drive B.
2. Do a warm boot and enter the date and time.
3. TYPE: **PATH A:** <ENTER>
4. TYPE: **PROMPT PG** <ENTER>
5. TYPE: **B:** <ENTER>
    [DOS will display the following prompt:]

```
B:\>
```

6. If you have any files on the disk in drive B, delete them all.

Create a Subdirectory

The MD command is used to create a subdirectory. If you do not provide a drive parameter, the subdirectory will be created on the default drive.

1. TYPE: **MD\WP** <ENTER>
    [Creates a subdirectory named \WP on drive B.]
2. TYPE: **DIR** <ENTER>
    [Your screen should match the following display:]

```
Volume in drive B is {Your last name}
Directory of B:\

WP            <DIR>        12-31-92   7:36p
```

3. TYPE: **CD\WP** <ENTER>
    [Changes the current subdirectory to \WP. Your prompt should now be B:\WP>.]
4. TYPE: **DIR** <ENTER>
    [Your screen should match the following display:]

```
Directory of B:\WP

.              <DIR         12-31-92    7:36p
..             <DIR>        12-31-92    7:36p
```

5. TYPE: **CD** <ENTER>
   [Changes the current directory to the root directory. Your prompt should now be B:\>.]
6. TYPE: **CLS** <ENTER>

Create the \WP\OLDLTR Subdirectory

1. TYPE: **MD\WP\OLDLTR** <ENTER>
   [Creates a subdirectory called \WP\OLDLTR.]
2. TYPE: **CD\WP** <ENTER>
   [Changes the current subdirectory to \WP. Your prompt should now be B:\WP>.]
3. TYPE: **DIR** <ENTER>
   [Your screen should match the following display:]

```
Directory of B:\WP

.              <DIR>        12-31-92    7:36p
..             <DIR>        12-31-92    7:36p
OLDLTR         <DIR>        12-31-92    7:36p
```

4. TYPE: **CD\WP\OLDLTR** <ENTER>
   [Changes the current subdirectory to \WP\OLDLTR. Your prompt should now be B:\WP\OLDLTR>.]
5. TYPE: **CD..** <ENTER>
   [Changes the current subdirectory to \WP. Your prompt should now be B:\WP>.]
6. TYPE: **CD..** <ENTER>
   [Moves up one directory to the root directory. Your prompt should now be B:\>.]
7. TYPE: **CLS** <ENTER>

Copy Files into a Subdirectory

1. TYPE: **COPY A:COMMAND.COM \WP** <ENTER>
   [Copies the file COMMAND.COM from drive A to the subdirectory \WP on drive B. DOS should list 1 file(s) copied if the copy was successful.]
2. TYPE: **DIR\WP** <ENTER>
   [Your screen should match the following display:]

```
Directory of B:\WP

.              <DIR>        12-31-92    7:36p
..             <DIR>        12-31-92    7:36p
OLDLTR         <DIR>        12-31-92    7:36p
COMMAND.COM    25276         7-18-88   12:00a
```

3. TYPE: **CLS** <ENTER>

Create Other Directories

1. Make sure that the default drive is set to drive B.
2. Make sure that the current directory is the root directory.
3. TYPE: **MD\LOTUS** <ENTER>
4. TYPE: **MD\DBASE** <ENTER>
5. TYPE: **MD\NULL** <ENTER>
6. TYPE: **DIR** <ENTER>
   [Your screen should match the following display:]

```
Directory of B:\

WP       <DIR>     12-31-92    7:36p
LOTUS    <DIR>     12-31-92    7:36p
DBASE    <DIR>     12-31-92    7:36p
NULL     <DIR>     12-31-92    7:36p
```

7. TYPE: **CD\NULL** <ENTER>
   [Changes the current subdirectory to \NULL. Your prompt should now be B:\NULL>.]
8. TYPE: **DIR** <ENTER>
   [Your screen should match the following display:]

```
Directory of B:\NULL

.      <DIR>     12-31-92    7:36p
..     <DIR>     12-31-92    7:36p
```

9. TYPE: **CD** <ENTER>
   [Changes the current directory to the root directory. Your prompt should now be B:\>.]
10. TYPE: **COPY \WP\COMMAND.COM \NULL** <ENTER>
    [This command copies COMMAND.COM from the \WP subdirectory to the \NULL subdirectory.]
11. TYPE: **CD\NULL** <ENTER>
    [Changes the current subdirectory to \NULL. Your prompt should now be B:\NULL>.]
12. TYPE: **DIR** <ENTER>
    [Your screen should match the following display:]

```
Directory of B:\NULL

.              <DIR>         12-31-92      7:36p
..             <DIR>         12-31-92      7:36p
COMMAND   COM  25276          7-18-88      1:43p
```

Remove a Subdirectory

The RD command is used to remove a subdirectory. Before the subdirectory can be removed, it must be emptied of all files and other subdirectories.

1. **TYPE: DEL *.* <ENTER>**
   [This command will delete all the files in the subdirectory \NULL. DOS will display the following prompt:]

```
ARE YOU SURE (Y/N)?
```

2. **TYPE: Y <ENTER>**
3. **TYPE: DIR <ENTER>**
   [Your screen should match the following display:]

```
Directory of B:\NULL

.              <DIR>         12-31-92      7:36p
..             <DIR>         12-31-92      7:36p
```

4. **TYPE: CD\ <ENTER>**
   [Your prompt should now be B:\>.]
5. **TYPE: RD\NULL <ENTER>**
   [Removes the subdirectory \NULL.]
6. **TYPE: DIR <ENTER>**
   [Your screen should match the following display:]

```
Directory of B:\

WP             <DIR>         12-31-92      7:36p
LOTUS          <DIR>         12-31-92      7:36p
DBASE          <DIR>         12-31-92      7:36p
```

7. **TYPE: CLS <ENTER>**

TREE Command

The TREE command displays a list of the subdirectories on the default drive.

1. TYPE: **TREE** <ENTER>
    [Your screen should match the following display:]

    ```
    SUB-DIRECTORIES: OLDLTR

    PATH: \WP\OLDLTR

    SUB-DIRECTORIES: NONE

    PATH: \LOTUS

    SUB-DIRECTORIES: NONE

    PATH: \DBASE

    SUB-DIRECTORIES: NONE
    ```

2. You have finished the tutorial. You may go back to the beginning of the floppy-disk users section on page 121 and repeat it, or you may do comprehensive problem six on page 130.

126 Subdirectory System

Hard-Disk Users

Startup

1. Do a warm boot.
2. TYPE: **PROMPT PG** <ENTER>
3. TYPE: **PATH C:\;C:\DT** <ENTER>
4. TYPE: **CD\DT** <ENTER>
   [DOS should display the following prompt:]

```
C:\DT>
```

5. If your prompt does not match the C:\DT> prompt, check with your instructor or computer center personnel and do not do any more steps until you have the C:\DT> prompt.
6. TYPE: **A:** <ENTER>
   [Your prompt should be A:\>.]
7. If there are any files on the disk in drive A, delete them all.

Create a Subdirectory

The MD command is used to create a subdirectory. If you do not provide a drive parameter, the subdirectory will be created on the default drive.

1. TYPE: **MD\WP** <ENTER>
   [Creates a subdirectory named \WP on drive A.]
2. TYPE: **DIR** <ENTER>
   [Your screen should match the following display:]

```
Volume in drive A is {Your last name}
Directory of A:\

WP              <DIR>        12-31-92    7:36p
```

3. TYPE: **CD\WP** <ENTER>
   [Changes the current subdirectory to \WP. Your prompt should now be A:\WP>.]
4. TYPE: **DIR** <ENTER>
   [Your screen should match the following display:]

```
Directory of A:\WP

      .              <DIR        12-31-92    7:36p
      ..             <DIR>       12-31-92    7:36p
```

5. TYPE: **CD** <ENTER>
   [Changes the current directory to the root directory. Your prompt should now be A:\>.]
6. TYPE: **CLS** <ENTER>

Create the \WP\OLDLTR Subdirectory

1. TYPE: **MD\WP\OLDLTR** <ENTER>
   [Creates a subdirectory called \WP\OLDLTR.]
2. TYPE: **CD\WP** <ENTER>
   [Changes the current subdirectory to \WP. Your prompt should now be A:\WP>.]
3. TYPE: **DIR** <ENTER>
   [Your screen should match the following display:]

```
Directory of A:\WP

 .              <DIR>         12-31-92    7:36p
 ..             <DIR>         12-31-92    7:36p
 OLDLTR         <DIR>         12-31-92    7:36p
```

4. TYPE: **CD\WP\OLDLTR** <ENTER>
   [Changes the current subdirectory to \WP\OLDLTR. Your prompt should now be A:\WP\OLDLTR>.]
5. TYPE: **CD..** <ENTER>
   [Changes the current subdirectory to \WP. Your prompt should now be A:\WP>.]
6. TYPE: **CD..** <ENTER>
   [Moves up one directory to the root directory. Your prompt should now be A:\>.]
7. TYPE: **CLS** <ENTER>

Copy Files into a Subdirectory

1. TYPE: **COPY C:\DT\COMMAND.COM \WP** <ENTER>
   [Copies the file COMMAND.COM from drive C to the subdirectory \WP on drive A. DOS should list 1 file(s) copied if the copy was successful.]
2. TYPE: **DIR\WP** <ENTER>
   [Your screen should match the following display:]

```
Directory of A:\WP

 .              <DIR>         12-31-92    7:36p
 ..             <DIR>         12-31-92    7:36p
 OLDLTR         <DIR>         12-31-92    7:36p
 COMMAND.COM     25276         7-18-88   12:00a
```

3. TYPE: **CLS** <ENTER>

Create Other Directories

1. Make sure that the default drive is set to drive A.
2. Make sure that the current directory is the root directory.
3. TYPE: **MD\LOTUS** <ENTER>
4. TYPE: **MD\DBASE** <ENTER>
5. TYPE: **MD\NULL** <ENTER>

128 Subdirectory System

6.   TYPE: **DIR** <ENTER>
[Your screen should match the following display:]

```
Directory of A:\

WP              <DIR>           12-31-92        7:36p
LOTUS           <DIR>           12-31-92        7:36p
DBASE           <DIR>           12-31-92        7:36p
NULL            <DIR>           12-31-92        7:36p
```

7.   TYPE: **CD\NULL** <ENTER>
[Changes the current subdirectory to \NULL. Your prompt should now be A:\NULL>.]
8.   TYPE: **DIR** <ENTER>
[Your screen should match the following display:]

```
Directory of A:\NULL

.               <DIR>           12-31-92        7:36p
..              <DIR>           12-31-92        7:36p
```

9.   TYPE: **CD** <ENTER>
[Changes the current directory to the root directory. Your prompt should now be A:\>.]
10.   TYPE: **COPY \WP\COMMAND.COM \NULL** <ENTER>
[This command copies COMMAND.COM from the \WP subdirectory to the \NULL subdirectory.]
11.   TYPE: **CD\NULL** <ENTER>
[Changes the current subdirectory to \NULL. Your prompt should now be A:\NULL>.]
12.   TYPE: **DIR** <ENTER>
[Your screen should match the following display:]

```
Directory of A:\NULL

.               <DIR>           12-31-92        7:36p
..              <DIR>           12-31-92        7:36p
COMMAND  COM    25276           7-18-88         1:43p
```

Remove a Subdirectory

The RD command is used to remove a subdirectory. Before the subdirectory can be removed, it must be emptied of all files and other subdirectories.

1.   TYPE: **DEL *.*** <ENTER>
[This command will delete all the files in the subdirectory \NULL. DOS will display the following prompt:]

```
ARE YOU SURE (Y/N)?
```

2. TYPE: **Y** <ENTER>
3. TYPE: **DIR** <ENTER>
   [Your screen should match the following display:]

```
Directory of A:\NULL

.           <DIR>       12-31-92      7:36p
..          <DIR>       12-31-92      7:36p
```

4. TYPE: **CD** <ENTER>
   [Your prompt should now be A:\>.]
5. TYPE: **RD\NULL** <ENTER>
   [Removes the subdirectory \NULL.]
6. TYPE: **DIR** <ENTER>
   [Your screen should match the following display:]

```
Directory of A:\

WP          <DIR>       12-31-92      7:36p
LOTUS       <DIR>       12-31-92      7:36p
DBASE       <DIR>       12-31-92      7:36p
```

7. TYPE: **CLS** <ENTER>

TREE Command

The TREE command displays a list of the subdirectories on the default drive.

1. TYPE: **TREE** <ENTER>
   [Your screen should match the following display:]

```
          SUB-DIRECTORIES: OLDLTR

          PATH: \WP\OLDLTR

          SUB-DIRECTORIES: NONE

          PATH: \LOTUS

          SUB-DIRECTORIES: NONE

          PATH: \DBASE

          SUB-DIRECTORIES: NONE
```

2. You have finished the tutorial. You may go back to the beginning of hard-disk users section on page 126 and repeat it, or you may do comprehensive problem six.

Comprehensive Problem Six

Floppy-Disk Users

1. If there are any files on the disk in drive B, erase them all. If there are any directories on the disk in drive B, erase them all. Make sure that you have a volume label of the first eleven characters of your last name on the data disk.
2. Make sure the current directory is B:\.
3. Create a directory called HOTDOG on the disk in drive B.
4. Make HOTDOG the current directory.
5. Create a subdirectory called MUSTARD on the disk in drive B.
6. Make the root directory the current directory.
7. Copy the file SYS.COM from drive A to the MUSTARD subdirectory on drive B.
8. Use the DIR/W > PRN command to print a directory of drive B.
9. Use the TREE/F command to print a display of the subdirectory system on drive B. Your printout should match the following display. If your printout matches the display, turn it in as comprehensive problem six.

```
Volume in drive B is {Your last name}
Directory of B:\

HOTDOG

DIRECTORY PATH LISTING FOR VOLUME {Your Last Name}

FILES:          NONE
PATH: \HOTDOG
SUBDIRECTORIES: MUSTARD
FILES:          NONE
PATH: \HOTDOG\MUSTARD
SUBDIRECTORIES: NONE
FILES:          SYS     .COM
```

Hard-Disk Users

1. If there are any files on the disk in drive A, erase them all. If there are any directories on the disk in drive A, erase them all. Make sure that there is a volume label of the first eleven characters of your last name on the data disk.
2. Make sure the current directory is A:\.
3. Create a directory called HOTDOG on the disk in drive A.
4. Make HOTDOG the current directory.
5. Create a subdirectory called MUSTARD on the disk in drive A.
6. Make the root directory the current directory.
7. Copy the file SYS.COM from drive C to the MUSTARD subdirectory on drive A.
8. Use the DIR/W > PRN command to print a directory of drive A.
9. Use the TREE/F command to print a display of the subdirectory system on drive A. Your printout should match the following display. If your printout matches the display, turn it in as comprehensive problem six.

```
Volume in drive A is {Your last name}
Directory of A:\

HOTDOG

DIRECTORY PATH LISTING FOR VOLUME {Your Last Name}

FILES:          NONE
PATH: \HOTDOG
SUBDIRECTORIES: MUSTARD
FILES:          NONE
PATH: \HOTDOG\MUSTARD
SUBDIRECTORIES: NONE
FILES:          SYS     .COM
```

Batch Files

Chapter 7

Learning Objectives

After completing chapter seven you will be able to:

```
1.   Define the purpose of Batch files.
2.   Define the purpose of an AUTOEXEC.BAT file.
3.   Use the COPY CON: command to create an ASCII file.
4.   Execute an AUTOEXEC.BAT file.
5.   Use EDLIN to create and edit an ASCII file.
6.   Use the TYPE command to display an ASCII file.
```

Batch Files

A **batch file** is an ASCII file that contains DOS commands and has a (.BAT) extension. Batch files are used to automatically execute DOS commands in sequential order. A **batch command** is the name of a batch file entered at the DOS prompt. If you consistently enter a series of commands to do a task, these commands can be captured in a batch file and the series of commands can be sequentially executed by typing the name of the batch file. The batch file becomes your own custom DOS command to do tasks that are unique to your own application of the microcomputer. When the batch files are created they must be given an extension of BAT (for example, W.BAT). To execute a batch file called W.BAT, type W and press <ENTER>. DOS will then automatically execute the commands in the W.BAT file. An example of a batch file is one that could be used to start an application program. For example, if the WordPerfect program is stored on the hard disk in the /WP directory, the following two commands would be used to start WordPerfect:

These two commands would take nine keystrokes (including pressing <ENTER> twice). A batch file called W.BAT can be created that would contain these two commands. To start WordPerfect using the batch file you would type W (do not type the extension) and press <ENTER>. DOS would then execute the steps in the batch file in the order in which they were entered. Each time this batch file is used, seven keystrokes are saved. Batch files are executed faster than you can type the commands yourself and the batch file will never make a typing error. Using batch files can automate and speed up your system significantly. It is a lot easier to teach other users of the system to enter W rather than teaching them how to change to the WordPerfect directory and then enter the WP command.

Stopping a Batch File

To start a batch file executing, type the name of the file without the BAT extension. Occasionally you will have to terminate a batch file because it is not executing correctly. The <CTRL-C> sequence will cancel the execution of a batch file. If you cancel the execution of a batch file by pressing <CTRL-C>, DOS will make you confirm this action by displaying the following prompt:

```
TERMINATE BATCH JOB (Y/N)?
```

You must respond with a Y and press <ENTER> to terminate the batch file.

Storing Batch Files

Batch files should be stored in the root directory of the hard disk and then the PATH command should include C:\ as part of the extended path. Since a batch file becomes a DOS command, the PATH command will search the named directories for DOS commands or batch files. You could then start WordPerfect from any subdirectory on the hard disk by typing W and pressing <ENTER>.

Batch File File Names

The name given to a batch file cannot be the same as the name of a DOS command. If you type the name of a batch file (for example, W) and press <ENTER> DOS will do the following steps:

```
1. DOS will first match the batch file name with the list of
   DOS internal commands.  If it matches any of the internal
   commands, DOS will execute the internal command.
2. If the batch file name doesn't match any of the internal
   commands, DOS will then match it against its list of external
   commands.  If the name matches any of the external commands
   DOS will execute the external command.
3. If the name does not match the name of any DOS command, DOS
   will search for the batch file on disk and will execute it.
```

Creating Batch Files

Batch files can be created using a word processing program if the program can output the file as an ASCII file (also called a text file). A batch file must be an ASCII file, which is a file without the special control characters that are added by most word processors to files that they create. You can also create ASCII files using **EDLIN**, the DOS text editor. Very short ASCII files can be created from the keyboard using the **COPY CON:** command.

AUTOEXEC.BAT File

You usually need to issue several DOS commands every time you boot DOS. For example, you need to set an extended path with the PATH command and you may want to use PROMPT to create a custom prompt. A batch file called AUTOEXEC.BAT (AUTOmatic EXECution) can be created to store a series of commands and have them automatically executed when DOS is booted. When DOS is booted a ROM program searches for an AUTOEXEC.BAT file in the root directory of the boot disk (A:\ on a floppy system and C:\ on a hard-disk system). The command PATH A:\ (for a floppy-disk system) or PATH C:\;C\DOS (for a hard-disk system) should be included in the AUTOEXEC.BAT file. On a floppy-disk system, the PATH A:\ command would allow you to issue DOS external commands from drive B. On a hard-disk system, the PATH C:\;C:\DOS would allow you to issue batch file commands from any subdirectory (the batch files would all be stored in the root directory of C:\) and issue DOS external commands from any directory because a path has been set to the C:\DOS subdirectory which will contain the external DOS commands.

Batch files should always be stored in the root directory but your system may have another name for the directory that stores the DOS external commands. If you are using a hard disk the PROMPT PG command should be included in the AUTOEXEC.BAT file so that the DOS prompt will display the current directory. If the AUTOEXEC.BAT file is present, DOS will bypass the automatic prompting for the date and the time. If your system has a battery-powered clock it may automatically enter the date and time or you may have to include a command to extract the date and time from the clock. If your system does not have a battery-powered clock, you will have to include the DATE and TIME commands in the AUTOEXEC.BAT file.

COPY CON:

Batch files can be created directly from the keyboard using the COPY CON: command. CON is the DOS system device name for the console (keyboard) and COPY CON: is followed by the name of the file that you want to create from the keyboard. This technique is appropriate for short files (one to three commands) and can be used to create other ASCII files such as CONFIG.SYS. Since batch files should be stored in the root directory of the boot drive, you should change directories to C:\ on a hard-disk system or A:\ on a floppy-disk system before you create the file. To create a batch file called AUTOEXEC.BAT from the keyboard, enter the following command:

```
COPY CON: AUTOEXEC.BAT
```

After entering COPY CON: AUTOEXEC.BAT and pressing <ENTER>, DOS will pause and wait for you to enter the command or commands that will be in your AUTOEXEC.BAT file. You will type the following:

```
PROMPT $P$G
```

You *will not* press <ENTER> after typing this command. Since this is the only command that will be put into this batch file, DOS must be told to end the file and write it to disk. Pressing the <F6> function key ends the creation of an ASCII file from the keyboard. When <F6> is pressed, DOS will display a ^Z (control Z) on the screen to indicate that it has created an end-of-file marker for the ASCII file. DOS then writes the AUTOEXEC.BAT file to the root directory of the disk and returns to the system prompt. Press <CTRL-ALT-DEL> to boot DOS, and as part of the booting process the AUTOEXEC.BAT file will be read by DOS and executed. The PROMPT command will be executed, and your system prompt will now display the default drive and the current directory.

EDLIN

COPY CON: is only appropriate for short files because you cannot edit the file to correct errors. If you make any errors, you must retype the entire file. To create longer files you should use either EDLIN or a word processor. EDLIN is very primitive compared to any word processor but it has two advantages. It is always present on any system because it is part of DOS and it always creates an ASCII file. You may be working on a system that does not contain your favorite word processor and you would be forced to use EDLIN to create an ASCII file. In the rest of this chapter examples will be given using EDLIN to either create a new ASCII file or modify an existing file. EDLIN can be used to add, delete, or change lines in any ASCII file. EDLIN cannot be used to edit DOS command files such as CHKDSK.COM or data files created by application programs because these files contain special characters that cannot be entered from the keyboard. ASCII files only contain characters that can be entered from the keyboard.

Creating Batch Files With EDLIN

EDLIN displays a command prompt of an asterisk (*). Whenever you are using DOS you will have a command prompt of A>, B>, or C>. A common error is to attempt to issue DOS commands when you are in EDLIN or issue EDLIN commands when you are in DOS. Examine the prompt to determine which program has control of the system. When you are editing a file using EDLIN it displays a number at the beginning of each line in the file. The following is a display of a file that you are editing with EDLIN:

```
1:*    PROMPT $P$G
2:     PATH A:\
```

The line numbers are used to select which line is to be changed or deleted. The line numbers are also used to choose an insertion position for lines that you wish to add to the file. As new lines are added or deleted, existing lines will be renumbered. The **current line** is denoted by an asterisk (*) immediately following the line number and indicates the location of the last change to the file. DOS has a current disk drive and a current directory and EDLIN has a current line. Most EDLIN commands consist of a single letter (L for list, I for insert, and D for delete). The command may be prefaced by a line number parameter to indicate which line or lines the command is to apply to. If you enter an EDLIN command without a line number parameter, the current line is used by default. EDLIN commands may be entered in uppercase or lowercase or a combination of uppercase and lowercase. The following table summarizes the important EDLIN commands where n, n1, and n2 are used to specify line numbers:

Command	Function
[n]I	Puts EDLIN into the insert mode and inserts lines of text before line [n]. If #I is entered, lines will be inserted after the last line in the file. Pressing <CTRL-C> terminates the insert mode and returns to the asterisk prompt. When you are creating a new file, you must enter I to begin inserting lines into the file.
[n1][,n2]L	Lists lines n1 through n2 on the screen. When n2 is omitted, lines n1 to the end of the file are listed. When L is used with no line numbers, the entire file is listed.
[n1][,n2]D	Deletes lines n1 through n2. If n2 is omitted only the line number entered is deleted. If n1 and n2 are omitted the current line is deleted.
E	Saves the file and returns to DOS.
Q	Returns to DOS without saving the file.
n	Directs Edlin to display a given line and lets you change it on the line below where it is displayed.

EDLIN commands

To use EDLIN to create a batch file the command EDLIN {filename} would be entered, where filename can be any filename with the extension (.BAT). To create a file called AUTOEXEC.BAT the following command would be entered:

```
EDLIN AUTOEXEC.BAT
```

EDLIN will then display the following screen:

```
New file
*
```

The asterisk (*) prompt indicates that you have left DOS and are using EDLIN. To begin inserting lines into a new file you must use the **I (Insert) EDLIN command**. If you enter I, EDLIN will display the following line:

```
1:*
```

This display shows that you are inserting line number 1 to the file. The asterisk following the line indicates that this line is the current line. To add a line type the line and press <ENTER>. For example, if you typed PROMPT PG and pressed <ENTER> EDLIN would display the following line:

```
2:*
```

The 2: indicates you are entering line 2 and the * indicates that line 2 is the current line. You will then type in the command PATH A:\ and press <ENTER>. EDLIN will then display the following line:

```
3:*
```

EDLIN is waiting for you to enter the third line in the file. Since you do not want to enter another line at this point you would press <CTRL-C> to return to the EDLIN prompt of *. If you entered the **L (List) EDLIN command**, EDLIN would list the following lines:

```
1:    PROMPT $P$G
2:*   PATH A:\
```

You want to add the CLS command before the first line in the file. To insert a line before an existing line in the file, preface the I command with the line number that you want to insert the line before. Since you wish to insert a line before line number 1, you would enter 1I and EDLIN would display the following line:

```
1:*
```

You would then type in CLS and press <ENTER>. After you press <ENTER> EDLIN would display 2:* to indicate that you can enter another line. You would press <CTRL-C> to end the insert mode and return to the * prompt. If you entered the L command, EDLIN would display the following lines:

```
1:     CLS
2:*    PROMPT $P$G
3:     PATH A:\
```

The **D (Delete) EDLIN command** is used to delete a line. To delete line one of the file, the following command would be used:

```
1D
```

If you listed the file after deleting line one EDLIN would display the following lines:

```
1:*    PROMPT $P$G
2:     PATH A:\
```

Notice that EDLIN renumbers the lines when you add or delete lines from the file. If you want to edit (change) a line, enter the line number of the line and press <ENTER>. The following command would be used to edit line two:

```
2
```

EDLIN would then display the following lines:

```
2: PROMPT $P$G
2:
```

The first line displayed (2: PROMPT PG) is called the the **template** and the second line displayed (2:) is called the new line. You can type in the new line or use the DOS editing keys to make your changes. When you finish editing the line press <ENTER> and the new line replaces the old line, and EDLIN returns to the * prompt. If you want to cancel the editing process without replacing the old line, press <CTRL-C>. To change a line you can use the DOS editing keys which are summarized in the following table:

Editing Key	Function
<F1> or <RIGHT ARROW>	Copies characters from the template to the new line, one character at a time.
<F3>	Copies all remaining characters from the template to the new line.
<BACKSPACE> or <LEFT ARROW>	Erases any characters that have been copied from the template.
<INS>	Toggles on the INSERT mode which allows you to add characters to the new line. Pressing <INS> again will toggle off the INSERT mode.
<DEL>	Skips over (does not copy) a character in the template.

DOS editing keys

The **E (End) EDLIN command** is used to save the file to disk and return to DOS. After you enter E the DOS prompt will be displayed.

Editing An Exiting File

If you wanted to edit (make changes to) the batch file you would enter the command EDLIN AUTOEXEC.BAT and press <ENTER>. EDLIN would display the following screen:

```
End of input file
*
```

The asterisk (*) prompt indicates that you have returned to EDLIN. When you edit an existing file you should begin by using the L command to list the file to determine the line numbers. If you listed the file EDLIN would display the following lines:

```
1:*    PROMPT $P$G
2:     PATH A:\
```

If you want to add a line to the end of the file you would enter the command #I and EDLIN would display the following line:

```
3:*
```

EDLIN is now in the insert mode and is waiting for you to add line 3 to the file. You can press <CTRL-C> to end the insert mode without adding a line. If you have made changes to your file that you wish to make permanent you must issue the E command to save your file. You wish to leave EDLIN without changing the file.

The **Q (Quit) EDLIN command** is used to return to DOS without saving the edited file. If you enter Q, EDLIN will make you confirm the Q command by displaying the following prompt:

```
ABORT   EDIT   (Y/N)?
```

If you press Y and then press <ENTER>, you will then return to DOS and the original file on disk will not be changed. If you press any other key you will remain in EDLIN.

Backup Files

When you use EDLIN to edit a file that has been previously saved on disk, EDLIN loads a copy of that file into RAM. The original file remains on disk. If you save the edited version of the file with the E command, EDLIN adds the extension .BAK to your original file and saves the edited file with the same name but without an extension of .BAK. For example, if you edited a file called X and then saved the edited file, your disk would contain a file called X and a file called X.BAK. The .BAK file can be used as a backup file. If for some reason you lose the X file you can then use the X.BAK file. You must rename the .BAK file to another filename without the .BAK extension before you can edit the backup file. If you do not wish to retain the backup files they can be deleted with the DEL command.

EDLIN Error Message

Problem: You are at the EDLIN * prompt and EDLIN displays the following error message:

```
ENTRY   ERROR
```

Solution: You attempted to enter a DOS command, for example, CLS, while in the EDLIN program. You must exit EDLIN before you can use DOS commands.

TYPE Command

The **TYPE command** is a DOS internal command used to display ASCII files. All batch files are ASCII files. You can use the TYPE command to display the AUTOEXEC.BAT file or any other ASCII file (CONFIG.SYS is also an ASCII file) on the screen. To display the AUTOEXEC.BAT file you would enter the following command:

```
TYPE AUTOEXEC.BAT
```

The TYPE command can only be used to display ASCII files, EDLIN, or some other text editor must be used to edit an ASCII file. Non-ASCII files can be displayed with the TYPE command but the display will be garbled and only partly readable. The following command using the output redirection operator can be used to print the AUTOEXEC.BAT file:

```
TYPE AUTOEXEC.BAT > PRN
```

REM Subcommand

There are several special DOS commands called **subcommands** that are primarily used in batch files. Several other subcommands will be covered in chapter eight. The **REM subcommand** is used to document a batch file. DOS reads and displays REM subcommands but it does not execute them. To add a REM subcommand to a batch file, use EDLIN or your word processor to edit the file. Type REM, press the <SPACE BAR> and then type in any text. The following is an example of a REM subcommand:

```
REM This is an AUTOEXEC.BAT file.
```

Terms

Batch command (132)
Batch file (132)
COPY CON: (133)
Current line (135)
D (Delete) EDLIN command (137)
E (End) EDLIN command (138)
EDLIN (133)
I (Insert) EDLIN command (136)
L (List) EDLIN command (136)
Q (Quit) EDLIN command (139)
REM subcommand (140)
Subcommands (140)
Template (137)
TYPE command (139)

Review Questions

Name _____

Mastery Self-Quiz True/False

Answer T for true or F for false.

1. ___ A batch file must have a .BAT extension.
2. ___ A batch file must be an ASCII file.
3. ___ To execute a batch file, type the file name (including the extension) and press <ENTER>.
4. ___ To cancel the execution of a batch file press <CTRL-S>.
5. ___ Batch files should be stored in the root directory of the boot drive.
6. ___ A batch file name should not be the same as a DOS internal or external command name.
7. ___ COPY CON: is used to type in a batch file from the keyboard.
8. ___ You can edit a batch file using COPY CON:.
9. ___ EDLIN can be used to create and edit a batch file.
10. ___ A word processor can be used to create and edit a batch file if it outputs an ASCII file.

Mastery Self-Quiz Fill-in

1. The EDLIN prompt is _____.
2. The _____ EDLIN command is used to insert lines.
3. _____ is used to end the EDLIN insert mode.
4. The _____ EDLIN command is used to list the file.
5. The _____ EDLIN command is used to delete lines.
6. The _____ EDLIN command would be used to delete lines two through four.
7. To edit line three of an EDLIN file you would type _____.
8. The _____ EDLIN command is used to end EDLIN and save the file.
9. The _____ EDLIN command is used to end EDLIN without saving the file.
10. The _____ command is used with output redirection to print a batch file.

Discussion Questions

1. When would you use COPY CON: to create a batch file?

2. List some commands that would be part of an AUTOEXEC.BAT file.

3. Discuss the creation and use of .BAK files created by EDLIN.

Chapter Seven Tutorial

If you are using a floppy-disk system, you will follow the steps labeled floppy-disk users. If you are using a hard-disk system, you will follow the steps labeled hard-disk users. If you are using a hard-disk system turn to page 146, otherwise do the instructions that follow.

Floppy-Disk Users

Startup

1. Insert the DOS system disk in drive A and insert the data disk (your disk) in drive B.
2. Do a warm boot and enter the date and time.
   [DOS will display the default prompt A>.]

Erase the Data Disk

1. TYPE: **B:** <ENTER>
2. Erase all files and directories from the data disk in drive B.
3. Take a directory of the data disk. There should be no files or directories on the disk.
4. TYPE: **COPY A:EDLIN.COM B:** <ENTER>
   [Copies the EDLIN program to drive B. DOS should display 1 file(s) copied.]

Create An AUTOEXEC.BAT File

The COPY CON: command is used to create an ASCII file from the keyboard. You will use the COPY CON: command to create an AUTOEXEC.BAT file. This AUTOEXEC.BAT file will change the DOS system prompt.

1. Make sure that you have the B> prompt.
2. TYPE: **COPY CON: AUTOEXEC.BAT** <ENTER>
   [This statement tells DOS to copy the information from the standard input device (keyboard) into the AUTOEXEC.BAT file on the default drive. DOS is now waiting for you to enter your file from the keyboard.]
3. TYPE: **PROMPT PG**
4. PRESS: **<SPACE BAR>** once
5. PRESS: **<F6>** <ENTER>
   [Pressing <F6> generates a Control-Z which ends the AUTOEXEC.BAT file. The message 1 file(s) copied should be displayed by DOS.]

Executing the AUTOEXEC.BAT File

You will now execute the AUTOEXEC.BAT file that you just created. The AUTOEXEC.BAT will change the DOS prompt from A> to A:\>.

1. TYPE: **AUTOEXEC** <ENTER>
    [This command causes the AUTOEXEC.BAT file to be executed. The last two lines displayed should match the following:]

```
B>prompt $P$G

B:\>
```

2. DOS has read your AUTOEXEC.BAT file and executed the PROMPT command to generate the custom prompt.
3. TYPE: **DIR/W** <ENTER>
    [DOS will display following files. Note the AUTOEXEC.BAT file.]

```
EDLIN     COM       AUTOEXEC  BAT
```

4. TYPE: **CLS** <ENTER>

Using EDLIN to Edit the AUTOEXEC.BAT File

The EDLIN program will be used to edit the AUTOEXEC.BAT file that you entered from the keyboard.

1. TYPE: **EDLIN AUTOEXEC.BAT** <ENTER>
    [EDLIN will display the following. The * prompt indicates that you are in EDLIN not DOS.]

```
End of input file
*
```

2. TYPE: **L** <ENTER>
    [You have entered the L (List) command. EDLIN will display the following listing of the AUTOEXEC.BAT file:]

```
        1:*PROMPT $P$G
*
```

144 Batch Files

3. TYPE: **#I** <ENTER>
   [The #I command tells EDLIN to insert a line at the end of the file. EDLIN will display the following:]

```
2:*
```

4. TYPE: **PATH A:** <ENTER>
   [EDLIN displays the following:]

```
        2:PATH A:\
        3:*
```

5. PRESS: **<CTRL-C>**
   [You have pressed <CTRL-C> to end the insertion mode. EDLIN should display the asterisk prompt in position 1 to indicate that you have left the insertion mode.]
6. PRESS: **L** <ENTER>
   [EDLIN responds with the following listing:]

```
        1: PROMPT $P$G
        2: PATH A:\
```

7. PRESS: **E** <ENTER>
   [You used the E command to exit EDLIN and save the file. DOS should display the following prompt:]

```
B:\>
```

TYPE Command

The TYPE command is used to type ASCII files on the screen or on the printer. An AUTOEXEC.BAT file is an example of a ASCII file. You must be connected to a printer to do this portion of the tutorial.

1. TYPE: **TYPE AUTOEXEC.BAT** <ENTER>
   [DOS will display the following:]

```
PROMPT $P$G
PATH A:\
```

2. TYPE: **TYPE AUTOEXEC.BAT > PRN** <ENTER>
   [DOS will type the AUTOEXEC.BAT file on the printer.]
3. You have completed the tutorial for chapter seven. You can repeat it, or you can do comprehesive problem seven on page 149.

Hard-Disk Users

Startup

1. Do a warm boot.
2. TYPE: **PROMPT PG** <ENTER>
3. TYPE: **PATH C:\;C:\DT** <ENTER>
4. TYPE: **CD\DT** <ENTER>
   [DOS should display the following prompt:]

```
C:\DT>
```

5. If your prompt does not match the C:\DT> prompt, check with your instructor or computer center personnel and do not do any more steps until you have the C:\DT> prompt.

Erase Data Disk

1. TYPE: **A:** <ENTER>
   [DOS should display the following prompt:]

```
A:\>
```

2. Be absolutely certain that you have the A:\> prompt before you do the next step.
3. Erase all files and directories on the data disk in drive A.
4. Take a directory of the data disk. There should be no files or directories on the disk.

Create An AUTOEXEC.BAT File

The COPY CON: command is used to create an ASCII file from the keyboard. You will use the COPY CON: command to create an AUTOEXEC.BAT file. This AUTOEXEC.BAT file will change the DOS system prompt.

1. TYPE: **COPY CON: AUTOEXEC.BAT** <ENTER>
   [This statement tells DOS to copy the information from the standard input device (keyboard) into the AUTOEXEC.BAT file on the default drive. DOS is now waiting for you to enter your file from the keyboard.]
2. TYPE: **PROMPT PG**
3. PRESS: **<SPACE BAR>** once
4. PRESS: **<F6>** <ENTER>
   [Pressing <F6> generates a Control-Z which ends the AUTOEXEC.BAT file. The message 1 file(s) copied should be displayed by DOS.]
5. TYPE: **DIR/W** <ENTER>
   [DOS will display the following directory listing showing that the AUTOEXEC.BAT file has been created:]

```
AUTOEXEC.BAT
```

Executing The AUTOEXEC.BAT File

To execute an AUTOEXEC.BAT file you can do a warm boot or enter the AUTOEXEC command. You are going to enter the PROMPT command with no parameters to cancel the custom prompt and then you will enter AUTOEXEC to have DOS read your AUTOEXEC.BAT file. When DOS reads the AUTOEXEC.BAT file, it will execute the PROMPT command in that file and restore the custom prompt.

1. **TYPE: PROMPT** <ENTER>
   [DOS will display the following default prompt:]

```
A>
```

2. **TYPE: AUTOEXEC** <ENTER>
   [DOS will display the following:]

```
A>PROMPT $P$G
A:\>
```

3. DOS has read the PROMPT PG command from the AUTOEXEC.BAT file and has restored the custom prompt.

Using EDLIN to Edit the AUTOEXEC.BAT File

The EDLIN program will be used to edit the AUTOEXEC.BAT file that you entered from the keyboard.

1. **TYPE: EDLIN AUTOEXEC.BAT** <ENTER>
   *[EDLIN will display the following. The * prompt indicates that you are in EDLIN not DOS.]*

```
End of input file
*
```

2. **TYPE: L** <ENTER>
   [You entered the L (List) command. EDLIN will display the following list of the AUTOEXEC.BAT file:]

```
        1:*PROMPT $P$G
*
```

3. **TYPE: #I** <ENTER>
   [The #I command tells EDLIN to insert a line at the end of the file. EDLIN displays the following:]

148 Batch Files

```
2:*
```

4. TYPE: **PATH C:\;C:\DT** <ENTER>
   [EDLIN displays the following:]

```
3:*
```

5. PRESS: **<CTRL-C>**
   [You have pressed <CTRL-C> to end the insertion mode. EDLIN should display the asterisk (*) prompt in position 1 to indicate that you have left the insertion mode.]
6. PRESS: **L** <ENTER>
   [EDLIN responds with the following listing:]

```
        1:  PROMPT $P$G
        2:  PATH C:\;C:\DT
```

7. PRESS: **E** <ENTER>
   [You have used the E command to exit EDLIN and save the file. DOS should display the A:\> prompt.]

TYPE Command

The TYPE command is used to type ASCII files on the screen or on the printer. An AUTOEXEC.BAT file is an example of a ASCII file. You must be connected to a printer to do this portion of the tutorial.

1. TYPE: **TYPE AUTOEXEC.BAT** <ENTER>
   [DOS will display the following:]

```
PROMPT $P$G
PATH C:\;C:\DT
```

2. TYPE: **TYPE AUTOEXEC.BAT > PRN** <ENTER>
   [The AUTOEXEC.BAT file will be printed.]
3. You have completed the tutorial for chapter seven. You repeat it, or you can do comprehensive problem seven.

Comprehensive Problem Seven

1. Add a REM statement with your name at the beginning of the AUTOEXEC.BAT file.
2. Add the DOS commands DATE and TIME as the last two lines of the AUTOEXEC.BAT file.
3. Use the TYPE command to print the AUTOEXEC.BAT file. The file should match the following:

```
REM Your Name
PATH A:\
PROMPT $P$G
DATE
TIME
```

Floppy-Disk Users

```
REM Your Name
PATH C:\;C:\DT
PROMPT $P$G
DATE
TIME
```

Hard-Disk Users

Subcommands And Hard Disk Commands

Chapter 8

Learning Objectives

After completing chapter eight you will be able to:

```
1.   Use the Subcommands ECHO, GOTO, and PAUSE in batch files.
2.   Use the hard disk commands PARK, FDISK, BACKUP, RESTORE,
     SYS, and REPLACE to maintain the integrity of a hard disk.
```

Subcommands

The following table summarizes the batch file subcommands:

Command	Action
@ECHO	Suppresses display of itself and the following batch-file commands. Version 3.3 or later.
ECHO ON/OFF	Toggles on/off the display of batch commands.
ECHO {Text}	Displays messages to the operator.
GOTO	Causes batch-file processing to continue on the line following a specified label.
PAUSE	Pauses the execution of a batch file.
REM	Documents the batch file.

DOS subcommands

These subcommands can be used to create batch files that will do more complicated procedures. For example, you have a computer with 3.5-inch 1.44MB high-density drive. You may use this drive to format a double-density diskette, so that you can use that diskette on a computer in another location that has double-density 3.5-inch drives. So that you, or co-workers, do not have to remember the syntax of this special formatting command, a batch file called DD.BAT can be created to do this task. The following batch file will format a double-density diskette, in a 1.44MB drive:

```
ECHO OFF
CLS
ECHO Insert double-density diskette in drive A:
ECHO Press <ENTER> when ready.
PAUSE>NUL
FORMAT A:/N:9/T:80
```

DD.BAT batch file

ECHO Subcommand

The **ECHO subcommand** can be used to toggle the display of the batch file commands on or off. The subcommand **ECHO OFF** instructs DOS to not display batch file commands as the batch file is run. The command ECHO OFF will be displayed but the rest of the commands will not be displayed unless the subcommand **ECHO ON** is used. Version 3.3 and greater of DOS provides the **@ECHO subcommand** which will even suppress the display of the ECHO command. For example, if @ECHO OFF was the first command in the DD.BAT file, the ECHO OFF command would not be displayed. The second command in the file is CLS which will clear the screen. The third command uses the ECHO command to display instructions to the operator. Even if an ECHO OFF command has been used, the ECHO command can be used to display text for the operator. The fourth command uses the ECHO command to display the text "Press <ENTER> when ready." for the operator. The fifth command uses the **PAUSE subcommand**. If the PAUSE subcommand is used by itself, it displays the message "Strike a key when ready ..." and pauses the batch file until a key is struck. The <CAPS LOCK>, <SHIFT>, and <CTRL> if struck, will be ignored by the PAUSE subcommand. To protect against someone using these keys, the message "Press <ENTER> when ready." is display above the PAUSE subcommand. The PAUSE subcommand is still used to pause the batch file and the redirection operator (>) is used to send the message "Strike a key when ready ..." to the NUL device which causes that message to <u>not</u> be displayed. The NUL (nonexistent) device is used when you want to discard output. The last command in the batch file uses the FORMAT command to format a disk in drive A as a 720KB disk. A complete novice can format a double-density disk in a 1.44MB drive by typing DD.

Replaceable Parameters

You may want a batch file to perform a slightly different operation each time you use it. The use of **replaceable parameters** can make a batch file more flexible. When you type the name of a batch file, you can add up to nine parameters following the batch-file name. DOS will assign **a variable name** to each of these parameters. In the batch file, you will use **a variable marker** numbered from 0 to 9 that will match up with the parameters used with the batch-file command. The variable marker 0 is not ordinarily used. Use only variable markers 1 through 9. The variable markers must be preceded with a percent sign (%) to instruct DOS that you are using replaceable parameters. The following batch file called BU.BAT will be used to illustrate the use of replaceable parameters:

```
COPY C:%1 A:%2
```

This batch file can be used to backup work done on the drive C to drive A without requiring the user to know the full syntax of the COPY command. For example, the user has completed work on a file called DOC and wants to copy this file to a backup disk in drive A. The following display shows the full syntax of the COPY command:

```
COPY DOC A:
```

Using the BU batch file, the user justs types the following and presses <ENTER>:

```
BU DOC
```

DOS will respond with the following display:

```
C>COPY C:DOC A:
1 file(s) copied
```

DOS will substitute DOC for the C:%1 replaceable parameter and since a second parameter was not specified with the batch file name, the default of A: will be used.

GOTO Subcommand

You may do a DOS process a number of times. The **GOTO subcommand** can be used in a batch file to repeat a repetitive process an unlimited amount of times. For example, you want to copy several files to a number of disks. The following batch file called DUP.BAT will use the GOTO subcommand to automate this process:

```
ECHO OFF
CLS
:START
ECHO Put a new disk in drive A to receive the documents.
ECHO To quit, type <CTRL-C> and press Y, or
ECHO Press <ENTER> when ready.
PAUSE<NUL
COPY DOC A:
COPY XXX A:
COPY ZZZ A:
ECHO Files have been copied.
GOTO START
```

DUP.BAT batch file

The GOTO subcommand is used to branch back to the beginning of the copying sequence so that it can be repeated. The GOTO subcommand must branch to a **label**. A label is a batch-file line that starts with a colon and is followed by a one-character to eight-character name. The label used in this program is :START. When the batch file first encounters the label :START in line three of the program, it just skips over the line. The ECHO subcommand is used to prompt the operator to put a disk in drive A to receive the documents. The fifth command tells the operator how to end the process and the sixth command will display the "Press <ENTER> when ready." prompt. The PAUSE<NUL subcommand pauses the program until a key is pressed and the three COPY commands copy the documents DOC, XXX, and ZZZ to drive A. The next command tells the operator that the files have been copied. The GOTO START subcommand directs the program to the label :START and the process is repeated. This program creates an endless loop which the operator can end when they have made enough copies of the documents by pressing <CTRL-C>, typing Y, and pressing <ENTER>.

Documenting Batch Files

The REM subcommand can be used to document batch-file programs. The REM subcommand will be displayed if you type the batch file to print but if ECHO is set to OFF, the REM subcommands will not display when the batch file is executing. The following batch-file program illustrates the use of the REM subcommand to document a batch-file program:

```
ECHO OFF
CLS
REM This batch file is used to make copies of files on
REM a series of diskettes.
:START
ECHO Put a new disk in drive A to receive the documents.
ECHO To quit, type <CTRL-C> and press Y, or
ECHO Press <ENTER> when ready.
REM The operator will either press <ENTER> to continue the
REM copy process, or will press <CTRL-C> to cancel.
PAUSE<NUL
COPY DOC A:
COPY XXX A:
COPY ZZZ A:
ECHO Files have been copied.
GOTO START
```

DUP.BAT batch file with documentation

Batch-file programs will often be modified at a later date. Include enough remarks so that either you or someone else could easily follow the program so that it could be modified.

Hard-Disk Commands

Most DOS commands can be used on either floppy diskettes or hard disks. A few commands such as DISK-COPY, can only be used on floppy diskettes. The commands that are typically only used on hard disks will be discussed in this section of the chapter. Floppy diskettes store data on a single floppy platter. Hard disks contain one or more rigid platters that are sealed within a unit to protect them from dust particles. The clearance between the read/write heads that transfer information to and from the hard disk and the platters is less than the size of a smoke particle. Because the clearance is so small, hard disks can suffer a disk crash. When the disk is powered on, the read/write heads float above the suface of the rotating disk platter. The read/write heads can crash into the platter. This can be caused by bumping the systems unit or by a temporary power outage when the disk is operating. If the hard disk crashes into an area where data is stored, that data will be lost. If the hard disk crashes into systems files (boot sector, directory sector, FAT table) the entire disk may be unreadable. Since a disk crash can occur, the hard disk must be backed up frequently.

PARK Command

Syntax: [D:]PARK

When a microcomputer is turned off, the read/write heads on many hard disks settle down on the surface of the disk. Over a period of time, this may damage the data on the disk. The **PARK command** is a DOS external command used to move the read/write heads to a vacant cluster just prior to turning off the power. Some hard disks are automatically parked when the microcomputer is powered down. If your hard disk does not automatically park itself, you should enter the PARK command just prior to powering down.

154 Subcommands and Hard Disk Commands

FDISK Command

```
Syntax: FDISK
```

Normally a hard disk will be preformatted and ready for use when you purchase it. The **FDISK command** is a DOS external command that would only be used if the manufacturer did not preformat the disk or it suffered a disk crash. Running the FDISK command is the first step required to prepare a hard disk for use. This command is executed with the DOS disk in drive A. When you enter the FDISK command, DOS will display a number of options. You will usually choose the option that is labeled as follows:

```
Creates DOS partition
```

DOS then asks if you want use the entire hard disk for DOS. If you do not plan to have any other operating system on the hard disk you will answer Y. If you plan to have other operating systems on the hard disk (for example, DOS and UNIX) you will answer N. Consult the DOS manual for procedures used to allocate partitions to operating systems other than DOS. After the DOS hard-disk partition is created, the FORMAT/S command must be used to prepare the hard disk to receive data. The /S option puts the DOS hidden files on the boot track of the hard disk. After the disk is formatted you will then copy COMMAND.COM to the root directory of the hard disk. The DOS external commands and utility programs will then be copied to a separate directory (for example, C:\DOS) on the hard disk. The hard disk is now ready for use. The PATH command will be used to set an extended path to the location of the DOS external commands on the hard disk.

Backing Up Hard Disks

The hard disk can fail when a temporary power loss causes the read/write heads to crash on the surface of the disk. You must frequently backup the data on the hard disk in case a crash occurs. DOS provides two commands to backup a hard disk: BACKUP and RESTORE.

BACKUP Command

```
Syntax: [D:][path]BACKUP [Source Drive][path][Filename[.ext]
<Target Drive> [/S] [/M] [/A] [/D] [/F]
```

The **BACKUP command** is a DOS external command used to copy hard-disk files to formatted floppy diskettes. Before you begin the backup procedure you need to format enough floppy diskettes to store the data on the hard disk. The diskettes should be labeled with a series of sequential numbers beginning with one. The numbered diskettes will be used in the backing up and restoring process. When BACKUP fills a diskette you will be prompted to insert a new diskette. You must label each diskette used in the backup process in consecutive order. The files are copied to diskette in a special compressed format. The following table shows the number of diskettes that will be required to backup all the files on a hard disk of a specified size:

Disk Capacity	Diskette Capacity			
	360KB	720KB	1.2MB	1.44MB
10MB	29	15	9	8
20MB	59	29	18	15
30MB	83	44	27	22
40MB	116	58	35	29
70MB	200	100	60	50

Floppy disks needed by BACKUP

If the hard disk fails, the COPY command cannot be used to copy the data back to the hard disk because the data is stored in the compressed format. The RESTORE command must be used to restore the data to the hard disk and the data must be restored in proper consecutive order designated by the numbered label on the floppy diskette. If you are using DOS Version 3.3 or higher, BACKUP will automatically format any new disks. The filename parameter can used to restrict the files that are backed up. Wildcard characters can be used with the filename parameter to further restrict the files that are backed up. The following table summarizes the options used with the BACKUP command:

Option	DOS Version	Action
/S	2.0 or later	Backs up files in subdirectories of the specified directory.
/M	2.0 or later	Backs up only files whose archive bit is turned on.
/A	2.0 or later	Adds files to be backed up onto the backup diskette without overwriting the original files.
/D	2.0 or later	Includes files created or modified on or after the date specified with the /D option.
/F	3.3 or later	Formats destination disks.

BACKUP options

If the **BACKUP /S (Subdirectory) option** is used, DOS will backup subdirectory files in addition to the files in the directory specified by the path parameter. The **BACKUP /M (Modified) option** can be used to backup only those files that have been modified since the last backup. DOS sets the archive bit on when a file is created or modified. The /M option will only backup those files that have the archive bit on and the archive bit is turned off after the file is backed up. The **BACKUP /A (Add) option** is used to add the files being backed up onto the existing backup disks without writing over existing files. The **BACKUP /D (Date) option** is used to backup any files that have been created or modified since a specified date. The following is an example of the a BACKUP command that will backup every file on drive C (including subdirectories) to floppy diskettes in drive A:

```
BACKUP C:\ A: /S
```

The following command will backup all files on the drive C (including subdirectories) that have been modified since the last backup:

```
BACKUP C:\ A: /S/M
```

The following command will backup all files on drive C (including subdirectories) that have been created since 12/31/91 and adds them to the target diskettes without erasing existing files on the target diskettes:

```
BACKUP C:\ A: /S/A/D:12/31/91
```

The following command will just backup the files in the \WP directory (and any subdirectries of \WP) on the source disk that have been modified since the last backup:

```
BACKUP C:\WP A: /S/M
```

The following command will just backup files with an extension of TXT in the \WP directory and any subdirectores of \WP that have been modified since the last backup:

```
BACKUP C:\WP\*.TXT A: /S/M
```

When you enter the BACKUP command, DOS will display a screen similar to the following screen:

```
Insert backup diskette 01 in drive A:

Warning! files in the target drive
A:\ root directory will be erased
Strike any key when ready
```

After you press <ENTER>, DOS will list the files that are being backed up until the diskette is full and it will then prompt you to insert diskette number 02. This process will continue until all the specified files have backed up. DOS Version 4 will automatically format any disks used by the BACKUP command.

RESTORE Command

```
Syntax: [D:][path]RESTORE <Source Drive> [Target Drive]
[Path][filename[.ext] [/S] [/P] [/M] [/N] [/A] [/B]
```

The **RESTORE command** is a DOS external command used to restore one or more files from diskettes created by the BACKUP command to the hard disk. RESTORE is only used if the contents of the hard disk have been accidentally erased or if the hard disk suffered a head crash. When multiple diskettes are involved, DOS will prompt you to insert the next sequential diskette. Wildcard characters can be used in the filename and extension parameters. The following table summarizes the options used with the RESTORE command:

Option	DOS Version	Action
/S	2.0 or later	Restores files in subdirectories of the specified directory.
/P	2.0 or later	Prompts user to confirm restoration of a read-only file or a file modified since the last backup.
/M	3.3 or later	Restores files modified since the last backup.
/N	3.3 or later	Restores files that no longer exist on the destination disk.
/A	3.3 or later	Restores files created or modified after or on the date specified with the /A option.
/B	3.3 or later	Restores files created or modified before or on the date specified with the /B option.

RESTORE options

The **RESTORE /S (Subdirectory) option** is used in the same manner as with the BACKUP command. It causes all subdirectories and their files to be restored to the hard disk. The following command will restore all files to the hard disk:

```
RESTORE A: C: /S
```

When the RESTORE command is used, DOS will display the following screen:

```
Insert backup diskette 01 in drive A:
Strike any key when ready
```

The same procedures as used with BACKUP are followed.

Updating DOS

SYS Command

```
Syntax: [D:][Path]SYS [D:]
```

The **SYS (SYStem) command** is an external DOS command that is used to copy the DOS system files (IO.SYS and MSDOS.SYS) from one disk to another disk. The SYS command is used to upgrade your hard disk to a new version of DOS without reformatting the disk. To upgrade DOS on your hard disk, boot DOS from the floppy containing the new version and then use SYS to transfer the hidden DOS system files to the hard disk. If DOS successfully copies the two hidden system files it will display the following message:

```
System transferred.
```

The next step would be to copy the COMMAND.COM file to the root directory of drive C. The final step would be to copy the DOS external commands and utility programs to the directory on your hard disk used to store these programs (usually C:\DOS).

REPLACE Command

```
Syntax: [D:][Path] REPLACE [Source Drive]<filename<.ext>
<Target Drive> [/S] [/A] [/D] [/P] [/R] [/W]
```

The **REPLACE command** is an external DOS command, available in DOS Version 3.2 or later, which can be used to update to a new version of DOS. This command can be used to copy the new version's external commands and utility programs to the hard disk. This command will replace all files on the destination drive that have the same filename on the source drive. The command can then be used with the REPLACE /A option, to add any new commands included in the new version of DOS to the directory on the hard disk. The following sequence of commands will replace and update the directory on drive C with the new versions of commands and with any new commands:

```
REPLACE A:*.* C:\DOS
REPLACE A:*.* C:\DOS /A
```

Terms

BACKUP command (154)
BACKUP /A (Add) option (155)
BACKUP /D (Date) option (155)
BACKUP /M (Modified) option (155)
BACKUP /S (Subdirectory) option (155)
ECHO OFF (151)
ECHO ON (151)
ECHO subcommand (151)
FDISK command (154)
GOTO subcommand (152)
Label (152)
PARK command (153)
PAUSE subcommand (151)
REPLACE command (158)
Replaceable parameters (151)
RESTORE command (157)
RESTORE /S (Subdirectory) option (157)
SYS (SYStem) (158)
Variable marker (151)
Variable name (151)
@ECHO subcommand (151)

Comprehensive Problem Eight

1. Using the DD.BAT file on page 150 as a guide, create a batch file that will format with a volume label a 5.25-inch double-density diskette in a high-density drive.
2. Use REM commands to document the batch file.
3. Floppy-disk users will format the disk in drive B and hard-disk users will format the disk in drive A.
4. The first command in the batch file should be a REM command listing your first and last name.
5. Use output redirection to print a copy of the batch file and turn in this copy.

Review Questions

Name _____

Mastery Self-Quiz True/False

Answer T for true or F for false.

1. ___ The ECHO subcommand can be used to toggle the display of batch file commands off.
2. ___ The @ECHO OFF command will suppress the display of itself.
3. ___ The PRN device is used if you want to discard output.
4. ___ The PAUSE command stops a batch file until the user presses a key.
5. ___ Variable markers must be preceded with a # sign.
6. ___ If ECHO is OFF, REM commands will not be printed.
7. ___ Some hard drives are automatically parked when the power is turned off.
8. ___ Variable markers are numbered from 0 to 9.
9. ___ The BACKUP command copies data to diskette in a special compressed form.
10. ___ It will take 200 360KB diskettes to backup a 40MB drive.

Mastery Self-Quiz Fill-in

1. The BACKUP _____ option is used to backup directories and their associated subdirectories.
2. The BACKUP _____ option is used to backup only those files that have their archive bit turned on.
3. The BACKUP _____ option adds files to backup disks without overwriting existing files.
4. The BACKUP _____ option is used to backup files that have been modified since a specified date.
5. The BACKUP _____ option automatically formats destination disks.
6. The _____ command is used to restore one or more files from diskettes created by BACKUP.
7. The _____ command is used to upgrade to a new version of DOS without reformatting the disk.
8. The _____ command is used to copy the external commands and utility files of a new version of DOS.
9. The GOTO subcommand must branch to a _____.
10. The _____ subcommand is used to document batch files.

Discussion Questions

1. Why should the PARK command be used?

2. Explain the use to the /S, /M, and the /D options of the BACKUP command.

3. Lists the steps necessary to upgrade to a new version of DOS on a hard drive.

Memory Types and CONFIG.SYS File

Appendix A

Expanded and Extended Memory

The original IBM PC used an 8088 microprocessor, a chip which could address a maximum of 1 million bytes (or one megabyte). DOS only allowed application programs to address 640KB of this 1MB space. As users created bigger documents and bigger spreadsheets, they demanded more memory space for their work. To address this problem Lotus, Intel, and Microsoft developed a **bank switching** scheme that allowed the use of the memory between 640K and 1 megabyte. This technique allow four banks of RAM to share this same space increasing the maximum memory available for application programs to about four megabytes. This memory was called **EMS (Expanded Memory Specification)**, **LIM (Lotus, Intel, Microsoft)**, or simply **expanded memory**. Lotus 1-2-3 Version 2, recognized this memory which allowed much larger spreadsheets to be created. A device driver is used to add this feature as though the expanded memory was a device. The 80286 microprocessor, introduced in 1984, could address up to 16 megabytes directly without any need for bank switching. IBM named this memory, the memory above the original 1MB, **extended memory**.

Unfortunately, this memory was only available when the 80286 processor was run in a special mode called the **protected mode**. Existing application programs could not be run in the protected mode so this extended memory was unavailable to them. Programming techniques were developed to allow the existing application programs to be run in the protected mode and eventually the extended memory became available for use. Most of the computers sold today are 286, 386, or 486 machines and they all have extended memory (memory above the original 1MB). The 386 and 486 machines can address up to 4 billion bytes (4 **gigabytes** or 4GB) of memory. Many application programs such as Lotus 1-2-3 Version 2, still only recognize expanded memory. To solve this problem, you can purchase a program such as QEMM, which can make extended memory look like expanded memory for those programs that only recognize expanded memory. If your machine has extended memory and the programs that you use recognize extended memory, your applications can be much larger. If your machine has extended memory but the programs that you use only recognize expanded memory, you will have to use QEMM or its equivalent to convert extended memory to expanded memory. DOS V4 has the XMAEM.SYS and XMA2EM.SYS driver programs that can switch extended memory to expanded memory. Because the banks of memory must be switched in and out, expanded memory is slower than extended memory.

CONFIG.SYS File

When DOS is booted, it loads the DOS system files into RAM and then DOS also searches the root directory of the boot drive for a file called CONFIG.SYS. The CONFIG.SYS file can be used to configure DOS for a particular system. If the CONFIG.SYS file is found, DOS executes the instructions in that file in sequential order, and modifies its configuration. If a CONFIG.SYS file is not found, DOS uses default values for its configuration. If you do not use database or accounting programs, you may not need to create a CONFIG.SYS file for your system. The CONFIG.SYS file is an ASCII file and can be created using COPY CON:, EDLIN, or any text processor that produces an ASCII file. The AUTOEXEC.BAT file (if present) is read and executed after the CONFIG.SYS file has been used to configure DOS. The CONFIG.SYS is typically used to modify the DOS data structures or provide special device drivers required by hardware devices connected to a system. **DOS data structures** are storage locations that it uses to keep track of items like open files and disk transfer buffers. **Device drivers** are software programs that are used by DOS to communicate with hardware devices such as the keyboard, mouse, screen, and printer. The CONFIG.SYS file contains a series of special commands called **directives**. These directives must be entered on separate lines in the file, and they are used to configure DOS to your particular system. The commonly used configuration directives are summarized in the following table:

Directive	Use
FILES	Sets the number of files that can be used at one time.
BUFFERS	Sets the number of disk buffers DOS uses.
DEVICE	Can be used to load a special screen manager called ANSI.SYS, load a driver program for a nonstandard device such as a mouse, load a driver program that will recognize an external disk drive, or create a RAM disk.

CONFIG.SYS directives

A typical CONFIG.SYS file for a system that uses a database program and a mouse may contain the following entries:

```
FILES=20
BUFFERS=15
DEVICE=MOUSE.SYS
```

The syntax for the CONFIG.SYS directives is as follows:

```
Directive=nn
```

The entry nn either specifies a number (for example, FILES=20) or specifies a device driver program (for example, DEVICE=MOUSE.SYS).

FILES Directive

```
Syntax: FILES=nn
```

The number of files specified (nn) must be in the range 8 to 255. The **FILES directive** specifies the maximum number of files that DOS can have open. DOS defaults to a value of FILES=8, but since DOS uses five of these files to handle the standard system hardware devices (keyboard, printer, screen and so forth), only three files can be opened by the user. Most systems should specify FILES=10. Since database programs open a large number of files, these programs usually recommend that you increase the FILES parameter to twenty. If DOS displays the error message "TOO MANY FILES OPEN", increase the number of files with the FILES directive.

BUFFERS Directive

```
Syntax: BUFFERS=nn
```

The **BUFFERS directive** specifies the number of disk buffers DOS creates in RAM. Prior to Version 4 of DOS, the number of buffers can range from one to ninety-nine. DOS will allocate 528 bytes in RAM for each buffer. DOS uses a default value of from two to fifteen depending upon the type of disk you have, the amount of RAM you have, and the version of DOS being used. The following table lists the default number of buffers for each system:

DOS Version	Buffers	Hardware
DOS prior to Version 3.3	2	Floppy-disk drives
	3	Hard Drive
Version 3.3 and later	2	360KB floppy drive
	3	any other hard or floppy drive
	5	More than 128KB of RAM
	10	More than 256KB of RAM
	15	More than 512KB of RAM

Number of buffers allocated

A **disk buffer** is a reserved area of RAM created by DOS to store information read from disk. RAM is much faster than disk memory. If you have configured your system with enough buffers, DOS will frequently find the information it needs in buffers, and since it will not have to access the disk, your application programs and DOS will run faster. When DOS reads data from disk, it reads the data in increments of a whole sector (512 bytes). Excess data not required from that sector is left in the buffer. If the excess data is needed later, DOS accesses it from the buffer, reducing the amount of disk access. DOS accumulates data to be written to disk in a buffer and DOS will only write to disk when the buffer is full. This also reduces the amount of disk access. When an application program closes a disk file or the program is terminated, DOS writes any information remaining in a buffer to disk. This activity is called flushing the buffer. When a disk buffer becomes either full or empty, DOS marks the buffer to indicate that it has been used recently. When DOS needs to reuse a buffer for new information, it uses the buffer that hasn't seen activity for the longest time. The buffering technique provides two advantages; DOS only reads and writes full sectors and by reusing the least-recently used buffers, DOS retains the data most likely to be needed next. Buffering allows DOS and your application programs to run faster. The number of buffers you should allocate depends on the application programs you use and how much RAM you have. The following list can be used to determine the correct number of disk buffers to allocate for your system:

> 1. If do not use accounting or database programs, allocate between ten and twenty buffers.
> 2. If a large number of subdirectories has been created, allocate from ten to twenty-five buffers.
> 3. If accounting or database programs are used, allocate from ten to thirty buffers.

Since each buffer takes 528 bytes, every two buffers take about 1KB of RAM. If you use large application programs and/or several terminate-and-stay-resident (**TSR**) **utility programs**, you may need to allocate a minimal number of buffers to fit everything within RAM. Even if you have enough memory, DOS Version 3.0 and later slows down if you allocate more than thirty buffers. This happens because DOS will spend more time searching the buffers for information than reading or writing to the disk. You must experiment with the number of buffers to see what is the optimum for your system. If you use a floppy-disk system, start with ten buffers; start with twenty buffers for a hard-disk system.

DEVICE Directive

> **Syntax: DEVICE=[D:][filespec]/options**

Each hardware device requires a device-driver program that DOS uses to communicate with the device. DOS provides default device drivers for the common hardware devices such as the keyboard, screen, and printer. DOS installs these standard drivers in memory each time the system is booted. Nonstandard devices, such as a mouse, may require a special device driver. Typically, the manufacturer of a nonstandard device will provide a device-driver program on floppy disk. To allow DOS to communicate with the nonstandard device, you must install the device drive each time DOS is booted. On floppy-disk systems device driver files should be stored in the root directory of the boot drive. On a hard-disk system, a special directory called \SYS should be created to store the driver programs. Assuming that you have a hard-drive system and have stored the driver program (typically called MOUSE.SYS) in the \SYS directory of the C drive, the following statement may be required if you have a mouse device:

> DEVICE=C:\SYS\MOUSE.SYS

ANSI.SYS

DOS also provides two device drivers that can be installed if needed. These device drivers are **ANSI.SYS** and **RAMDRIVE.SYS**. RAMDRIVE.SYS is called **VDISK.SYS** on PC-DOS systems. The ANSI.SYS driver provides enhanced keyboard and screen support. If you do not use ANSI.SYS, DOS will automatically takes care of controlling what appears on the screen. If you install ANSI.SYS, you can control more directly what appears on the screen. An application program may require that you install the ANSI.SYS driver in your CONFIG.SYS file with the following command:

> DEVICE=ANSI.SYS

RAMDRIVE.SYS

RAMDRIVE.SYS and VDISK.SYS are available on DOS 3.0 or later. These drivers are used to create a RAM disk or virtual disk. A RAM disk sets aside a portion of RAM to be used as an additional disk drive. A RAM disk is most useful if you do not have a hard disk. You can create a RAM disk which will operate at least ten times faster than a floppy disk. If you have an A and a B drive, the RAM disk will be drive C. Since the drive is created from RAM, you must save any work done on the RAM disk to an actual disk before you power down the system. The programs that you use and the amount and type of RAM that you have will determine whether or not you should use a RAM disk and how large it can be. If you have extended or expanded memory, the RAM disk can be created using that memory. If you have extended or expanded memory you can probably use a RAM disk. If you only have conventional memory, you probably will not have enough space for a RAM disk. For example, you have a computer with 640K of conventional memory. With Lotus 1-2-3 Release 2.2 and DOS loaded, only about 360KB will be available for worksheet creation. Space allocated to a RAM disk will reduce the size of the worksheet that you can create. With dBase IV and DOS loaded in the same machine, only about 170KB of memory will be free for a RAM disk. The syntax of the RAMDRIVE parameter is as follows:

```
DEVICE=[D:]RAMDRIVE.SYS size sectorsize numfiles [/X][/E]
```

The options are summarized by the following table:

Option	Use
Size	The size (in KB) of the RAM disk. Default is 64KB.
Sectorsize	The size (in bytes) of the RAM disk sectors. Default is 128KB but 256 or 512 can be used.
Numfiles	The maximum number of files that the RAM drive can store. The default is 64 but a value in the range of 2 to 512 can be used.
/E:max	Specifies that DOS should create the RAM drive in extended memory.

RAMDRIVE options

The **RAMDRIVE size option** can range from 1KB to the maximum amount of memory available minus 64KB that DOS requires for application-program space. For most 8088 machines, the maximum amount of memory is 640KB. The 286, 386, and 486 machines can have at least 16MB of RAM, so you could create more than one RAM disk on these machines. With DOS Version 3.2 or greater, DOS will automatically reduce the size of the RAM disk if you do not have the 64KB free that DOS requires for application program space. DOS Versions 3.0 and 3.1 will display an error message and fail to install the RAM disk if you do not have the 64KB free for application program space. Version 3.0 and 3.1 will also reduce your RAM disk to 64KB if you specify a size greater than the RAM installed in the machine. To maximize speed set the **RAMDRIVE sectorsize option** to 512 if you store large files on the RAM disk. If you store a series of small files on the RAM disk, set the sectorsize to 128 or 256 to maximize the use of space on the RAM disk. Set the **RAMDRIVE numfiles option** to the number of files that you expect to store on the RAM disk. If you have extended memory, use the **RAMDRIVE /E option** to direct DOS to put the RAM disk in extended memory. If you use the /E option, the maximum size of the RAM disk is 4MB.

DOS Version 3.0 does not have a max parameter. DOS Version 3.1 and greater use the **RAMDRIVE max parameter** to specify the maximum amount of sectors that can be transferred at one time from the RAM disk. Some programs, particularly communications programs, may lose characters when using a RAM disk. If this occurs set the max parameter to 7 or less, otherwise, specify a max parameter of /E:8. The following entry in CONFIG.SYS will create a RAM disk identical to a 360KB floppy with 360KB of memory, a 512 byte sector size, and space for 112 files:

```
DEVICE=RAMDRIVE 360 512 112
```

The following entry in CONFIG.SYS will create a RAM disk that uses all the extended memory on a computer with 1MB of RAM (384KB is the difference between 1MB of RAM and 640KB of conventional memory):

```
DEVICE=RAMDRIVE 384 512 112 /E:8
```

DRIVER.SYS

DRIVER.SYS is a device driver for disk drives. If you have an external floppy-disk drive or a non-standard hard-disk drive, you will have to use a DRIVER.SYS command in your CONFIG.SYS file. Many users have added either an external 3.5-inch drive to systems that had 5.25-inch internal drives, or they added an external 5.25-inch drive to systems that had 3.5-inch internal drives. The DRIVER.SYS program must be used to inform DOS about which type of external disk drive you have added to your system. Consult the DOS manual for the switches used with this command.

DOS Version 4

Appendix B

DOS Version 4

DOS Version 4 provides several important new features including the ability to install DOS with the SELECT program, a DOS Shell program that provides a menu-driven interface to select commands, and support for hard disks with more than 32MB of storage. The following table summarizes the new features of Version 4:

Feature	Use
SELECT Command	Used to install DOS and install the DOS Shell program.
DOS Shell	Provides a menu-driven interface that can be used to enter DOS commands and select applications programs to be run.
BUFFERS Directive	The /X option added to the BUFFERS directive in CONFIG.SYS allows disk buffers to be loaded into expanded memory and a new type of buffer called a look-ahead buffer can be used.
XMA2EMS.SYS	A new device driver for expanded memory.
XMAEM.SYS	Allows emulation of an expanded memory adapter on 80386 machines.
MEM Command	Provides a report on available conventional, extended, and expanded memory, and lists how much of each is unused.
FDISK Command	Supports hard disk larger than 32MB.

DOS Version 4 features

SELECT Program

The **SELECT utility program** is used to install DOS and the DOS Shell on the microcomputer. SELECT can be used to create system diskettes, and it can be used to copy DOS to the hard disk. You cannot use the SELECT utility to just install the Shell; you have to install both DOS and the Shell. The SELECT program is on the disk marked INSTALL.

168 DOS Version 4

Disks Larger Than 32MB

Prior to Version 4, DOS would only recognize a hard disk of up to 32MB. If you had a hard disk with more storage, the disk had to be formatted as if there were several disks on one physical disk, because no single disk could exceed 32MB. The Version 4 FDISK command allows disks to be formatted at more than 32MB.

DOS Shell

DOS Version 4 introduced a menu-driven user interface, called the **DOS Shell**, that can be keyboard-driven or mouse-driven. This interface allows the user to select commands from a list of options rather than having to learn each command. This interface helps new users because they can perform basic DOS functions without extensive training. You can load the DOS Shell from the DOS prompt or have it automatically loaded using the AUTOEXEC.BAT file. The syntax for starting the DOS Shell program is as follows:

```
DOSSHELL
```

DOSSHELL is an external command, which actually acts as a batch file. The DOSSHELL batch file is created when DOS is installed using the SELECT program. When you invoke the DOSSHELL batch file, it calls the Shell program and passes various parameters that specify the mouse type, the screen colors, and other options. Although the Shell program can handle the basic functions of DOS, not all commands are included in the Shell. In addition, for commands included, not all the options are always available. The command prompt is still necessary for more advanced use of DOS.

BUFFERS Directive

DOS Version 4 has added options to the BUFFERS Directive, used in the CONFIG.SYS file. These options to can be used if you have expanded memory. The buffers can be loaded into expanded memory. You can use up 10,000 buffers, and a new type of buffer called a **look-ahead buffer** can be used. The expanded syntax is as follows:

```
BUFFERS=buffers,look-ahead_buffers/X
```

The **BUFFERS directive /X option** tells DOS to load the buffers into expanded memory. Look-ahead buffers are special buffers that DOS uses to store sectors ahead of the sector requested by a DOS-read operation. You can specify from zero to eight look-ahead buffers. If you specify three look-ahead buffers, then every time DOS reads a sector from disk, it will also read the following three sectors. If your application or DOS needs one of the sectors already read, DOS retrieves the sector from the look-ahead buffer and does not have to access the disk. The default is one look-ahead buffer. The following directive tells DOS to allocate one thousand buffers, eight look-ahead buffers, and store them in expanded memory:

```
BUFFERS=1000,8 /X
```

XMAEM.SYS and XMA2EMS.SYS

DOS Version 4 provides two new device drivers, called **XMAEM.SYS** and **XMA2EMS.SYS**, that enable you to use expanded memory with your system. The drivers were designed for IBM memory adapters but may be usable with other brands. In some implementations of DOS Version 4, the XMAEM.SYS program is called **EMM386.SYS**. You can use the XMA2EMS.SYS driver if you have either an expanded memory adapter or an 80386 computer with the XMAEM.SYS driver installed. The XMAEM.SYS driver is designed to be used with 80386 systems. It enables you to use extended memory that can be addressed as though it were expanded memory. You use this driver to define the number of 16KB pages of extended memory to be devoted to expanded memory. The syntax of this directive is as follows:

```
DEVICE=XMAEM.SYS NN
```

NN is the number of pages of extended memory to allocate (divide the total extended memory by 16 to calculate this figure) to expanded memory. The XMAEM.SYS driver must be loaded before the XMA2EMS.SYS driver in the CONFIG.SYS file. Refer to the software and hardware manuals for your system to install these drivers properly.

MEM Command

DOS Version 4 provides a new command, the **MEM** command which calculates all types of memory on a particular system. MEM can be run to see how memory is configured between conventional, expanded, and extended memory. For example, on a machine with 640KB memory and an 2MB memory board, the MEM command might produce the following report:

```
655360 bytes total memory
655360 bytes available
569504 largest executable program size

1703936 bytes total EMS memory
1703936 bytes free EMS memory

524288 bytes total extended memory
524288 bytes available extended memory
```

Glossary

Appendix C

Adapter Cards: Installed inside the systems unit they are used to customize the microcomputer to your individual specifications.
Applications Programs: Programs that are used to accomplish a particular function.
Archive Bit: An attribute bit that is part of each file. This bit is turned on by DOS when a file is created or modified.
AUTOEXEC.BAT: A special batch file that is executed by DOS at boot time.
Backup: A copy of a file that can be used if the original file is destroyed.
Backup Diskettes: A diskette that can be used if the original diskette fails.
Bad Sectors: Areas of the disk that are marked as not usable by DOS.
Bank Switching: A technique used by expanded memory that allows several banks of memory to share the memory space between 640K and 1MB.
Batch Command: The name of a batch file entered at the DOS prompt.
Batch File: An ASCII file that contains DOS commands and has a (.BAT) extension.
Bit: Computer chips, including microprocessor chips, store information by assigning a value of either 0 or 1 to the smallest unit of storage, a binary digit.
Booting: The process of loading the DOS system into RAM.
Bootstrap Loader Program: A program stored in ROM that is used to boot DOS.
Boot Record Sector: An area on a disk that stores information about the format structure of the disk and contains the bootstrap program.
Bus: A common communications channel.
Byte: Eight bits grouped together.
Cold Boot: The process of turning on the computer to boot DOS.
Cluster: The smallest addressable location that is used to store data on a disk. Two sectors (one on each side of the disk) are combined to make up a cluster.
Computer Program: A set of commands that instructs a computer to perform a task.
CONFIG.SYS: A special file that can be created and changed by the user to configure the microcomputer system.
Current Directory: The default directory used by DOS if you do not specify a directory in a command.
Current Line: Marked with an *, this line is used by EDLIN to denote the last change to a file.
Cursor: A flashing dash that marks your current position on the screen.
Cylinder: See Cluster.
Daisy Wheel Printer: A letter-quality printer with a very slow output rate.
Data: The words or numbers processed by the microcomputer to create useful information.
Data Diskette: Has its entire surface reserved for data.
Data Files: Files used to store data.
Data Sectors: Areas on the disk used to store data.
Default: A value that DOS will use if you do not supply a value.
Default Drive: The drive that DOS is booted from.
Delimiter: A special character used to define the end of a portion of a DOS command.
Density The measure of the number of magnetic spots recorded in a one-inch area on a diskette.
Device Drivers: Software programs that are used by DOS to communicate with hardware devices.
Directory: Also called the root directory, this is an area on the disk used to store the names of files and the beginning location of files.
Directives: Special commands used in the CONFIG.SYS file.

Disk: A storage media used to record data.
Disk Buffer: A reserved area of RAM created by DOS to store information read from disk.
Disk Drives: The microcomputer's permanent memory device.
DOS Command: A character-string specification that references the name of a DOS program.
DOS Command Processor: COMMAND.COM which forms the interface between the user and DOS.
DOS Data Structures: Storage locations used to keep track of items like open files and disk transfer buffers.
DOS Editing Keys: Keys used to retrieve and edit the last DOS command issued.
DOS Prompt: The characters A> or C> that are displayed to indicate that DOS is ready to receive commands.
DOS System Files: MSDOS.SYS, IO.SYS, and COMMAND.COM in the MS-DOS system. IBMDOS.COM, IBMBIO.COM, and COMMAND.COM in the PC-DOS system.
Dot Matrix Printer: An inexpensive non-letter-quality printer.
Dot Pitch: The distance between the pixels on a screen.
Enhanced Keyboard: Released in 1986, it has more than one hundred keys.
Expanded Memory: Memory between 640KB and 1MB that can be used by application programs that recognize this memory.
Expansion Slot: Adapter cards are plugged into these slots.
Extended Memory: Memory above 1MB.
Extension: An optional one-to three-character tag than may be added to a filename.
External Commands: A series of DOS programs that must be retrieved from the boot drive when they are used.
File: A storage facility on disk used to record related information.
File Allocation Table (FAT): An area on disk that stores the location of bad sectors, identifies which sectors belong to which files, and which sectors can be used to store new data.
File Name: The filename and the extension.
Filename: A one-to eight-character name given to a file.
Filespec: Combines a disk-drive name and a file name.
File Specification: See Filespec.
Filter Commands: Used to take standard DOS output, modify it in some way, and then send it to the standard output device.
Fragmented Files: Files stored in noncontiguous clusters.
Gigabyte (GB): One billion bytes.
Global Filename Characters: See wildcards.
Hardware: The tangible, physical machinery.
Hidden Files: Files that are not shown in the directory listing.
Ink Jet Printer: A slightly less expensive alternative to the laser printer.
Input Buffer: The last DOS command entered is captured in this area of RAM.
Interlaced Scanning: The monitor takes two passes to create an image.
Internal Commands: The most commonly used commands and are retrieved from RAM when they are used.
Interrupt Signal: Pressing <CTRL-S> sends this signal to DOS which causes a command to pause until a key is pressed.
Keyboard: The primary input device on a microcomputer.
Keyboard Buffer: A memory unit that stores keystrokes.
Kilobytes (KB): 1,024 bytes of memory.
Laser Printer: The most popular letter-quality printer.
Lost Allocation Clusters: Parts of files that have been deleted from the directory, but are still recorded in the FAT.
Megabytes (MB): 1,048,576 bytes of memory.
Megahertz (Mz): One million cycles per second. It is a unit used to measure how fast the microprocessor clock runs.
Memory Chip: A physical unit used to store both RAM and ROM.
Microcomputer: An electronic device, controlled by instructions stored within its memory, that allows data to be entered, processed, outputted, and stored.
Microcomputer System: A collection of hardware components that work together.

Microprocessor Chip: The hardware device that does the processing.
Modem: A device used to communicate with other computers.
Monitor: A display screen used to view input to and output from a microcomputer.
Motherboard: A printed circuit board that forms the bottom of the systems unit.
Mouse: An input device that may be used in place of or in addition to a keyboard.
Noninterlaced Scanning: The screen image is created with only one pass.
Operating System Program: A program used to manage the computer system.
Options: Used to change the output of a command.
Original Keyboard: Introduced in 1981, this keyboard contains about eighty keys.
Parallel Port: Transfers data eight bits at a time.
Parameters: Modifiers of a command that usually indicate the target of the command.
Parent Directory: A directory that has one or more subdirectories created underneath it.
Path Symbol: The backslash character.
Pathname: Begins with a backslash and is used to steer DOS to the correct directory.
Peripheral: Every piece of hardware that is connected to the systems unit with an adapter card or a cable.
Piping: See Filter Commands.
Pixels: Picture elements that make up the monitor display screen.
Ports: Used to connect hardware devices to the system unit.
POST (Power On Start Up) Program: A program stored in ROM that is run when a cold boot is done. This program checks the machinery and issues an error message if a malfunction is found.
Printer: Hard copy output device.
Program Files: Used to store commands rather than data.
Protected Mode: A special mode of the 80286 microprocessor that allows extended memory to be used.
RAM: Random Access Memory.
Read-only File: A file that can be read but cannot be deleted or over-written.
Redirection: Changing the standard input and output device used by a DOS command to another input or output device.
Replaceable Parameters: Used to make a batch file more flexible.
ROM: Read Only Memory.
Root Directory: A directory that is created by DOS and is used to store the names of files and subdirectories.
Sectors: Pie-shaped areas on the disk that are used to store data.
Serial Port: Transfers data one bit at a time.
Software: The programs that tell the hardware what to do.
Subcommands: Special commands used primarily in batch files.
Subdirectories: Directories that are created by the user and are used to store the names of other subdirectories and files.
Subdirectory System: A series of subdirectories created by the user to organize a hard disk.
System: A group of elements that, when properly combined, produces a result.
System Diskette: Has the DOS systems files stored on it, making it a bootable diskette.
Systems Unit: A piece of hardware that contains the microprocessor chip, RAM, ROM, disk drives, and adapter cards.
Tape Backup Units: Used to provide backup storage for data on disk drives.
Template: The original line that is displayed when you are editing an line using EDLIN.
Toggle: Like a light switch, may be on or off.
Tracks: Circular areas on a disk that are used to store data.
TSR Utility Programs: Utility programs that terminate but stay resident in RAM so they can be restarted by pressing a special hot key.
Utility Programs: Programs that, when added to operating systems or application programs, provide additional flexibility or ease of use.
Variable Marker: Numbered from 0 to 9 and prefaced with the % sign, these markers are matched up with the replaceable parameters used in the batch-file command.
Variable Name: A name assigned by DOS to each replaceable parameter used in a batch-file command.

Vertical Scanning Frequency (VSF): The rate at which a complete screen is filled with an image.
Warm Boot: The process of booting DOS when the computer is already turned on.
Wildcard Characters: Characters (the * character and the ? character) used in DOS commands that can represent any other character.
Word: Bytes are grouped together (always in multiples of two) to form words.
Word Size: Determines how much data a computer can process at one time.
Write-protect Notch: On a 5.25-inch diskette a write-protect tab is placed over this area to write-protect the diskette.
Write-protected: A drive can read the diskette but it cannot write on it.
Write-protect Window: Can be opened to write-protect a 3.5-inch diskette.

Command Summary

Appendix D

DOS Editing Keys

Editing Key	Function
<F1> or <RIGHT ARROW>	Copies characters from the template to the new line, one character at a time.
<F3>	Copies all remaining characters from the template to the new line.
<BACKSPACE> or <LEFT ARROW>	Erases any characters that have been copied from the template.
<INS>	Toggles on the INSERT mode which allows you to add characters to the new line. Pressing <INS> again will toggle off the INSERT mode.
<DEL>	Skips over (does not copy) a character in the template.
<ESC>	Cancels the command.

Key Sequences

Warm Boot: <CTRL-ALT-DEL>
Pause the screen: <CTRL-S> or <PAUSE>
Cancel a Command: <CTRL-C> or <CTRL-BREAK>

Printing Commands

Print The Screen: <SHIFT-PRTSC> or <PRINT SCREEN>

Printer Redirection: {Command} > PRN
Example: DIR > PRN

Toggle the printer on/off: <CTRL-P>

System Information Commands

CLS Command

```
Syntax: CLS
```

CLS is an internal command used to clear the screen.

DATE Command

```
Syntax: DATE [mm-dd-yy]
```

DATE is an internal command used to change the system date.

DIR Command

```
Syntax: DIR [D:][filename[.ext]] [/P] [/W]
```

DIR is an internal command used to display a directory listing.

PROMPT Command

```
Syntax: PROMPT <Prompt String>
```

PROMPT is an internal command used to create a custom DOS prompt.

TIME Command

```
Syntax: TIME [hh:mm:[:ss]]
```

TIME is an internal command used to change the system time.

VER Command

```
Syntax: VER
```

VER is an internal command used to display the version of DOS in RAM.

Disk Management Commands

CHKDSK Command

```
Syntax: [D:]CHKDSK [D:][filename[.ext]] [/F] [/V]
```

CHKDSK is an external command that displays a disk status report for a specified disk and lists the internal memory status of a microcomputer.

FORMAT Command

```
Syntax: [D:]FORMAT <D:> [/V] [/S] [/4] [/T:xx] [/N:x]
```

FORMAT is an external command used to prepare a new disk for use.

LABEL Command

```
Syntax: [D:]LABEL [D:] [Volume Label]
```

LABEL is an external command used to add, change, or delete a volume label without reformatting the disk.

VOL Command

```
Syntax: VOL [D:]
```

VOL is an internal command used to display the volume label on a disk.

File Management Commands

ATTRIB Command

```
Syntax: [D:]ATTRIB [+R|-R] [+A|-A] [D:]filename[.ext] [/S]
```

ATTRIB is an external command used to prevent a file from being accidentally deleted.

COMP Command

```
Syntax: [D:]COMP [D:]filename[.ext]  [D:[filename[.ext]
```

COMP is an external command that is used to compare individual files.

COPY Command

```
Syntax: COPY [D:]<Source File Name> [D:][Target File Name]   [/V]
```

COPY is an internal command used to make duplicate copies of existing files.

DEL Command

```
Syntax: DEL [d:]filename[.ext]
```

DEL is an internal command used to erase files from a disk.

DISKCOMP Command

```
Syntax: [D:]DISKCOMP <Source Drive> <Target Drive>
```

DISKCOMP is an external command used to compare diskettes.

DISKCOPY Command

```
Syntax: [D:]DISKCOPY <Source Drive> <Target Drive>
```

DISKCOPY is an external command used to copy entire diskettes.

REN Command

```
Syntax: REN [d:]<Old File Name> <New File Name>
```

REN is an internal command used to change the filename of a file.

XCOPY Command

```
Syntax: XCOPY <Source filespec> [Target filespec> [/W] [/P]
[/D:mm-dd-yy] [/S] [/E] [/M]
```

XCOPY is an external command that can be used to copy selected files.

Directory Management Commands

CD Command

```
Syntax: CD [D:][PATH]
```

CD is an internal command used to change the current subdirectory on a particular drive.

MD Command

```
Syntax: MD [D:][PATH]<SUBDIRECTORY NAME>
```

MD is an internal command used to create subdirectories.

Path Command

```
Syntax: PATH [D:][path][;path][;path]
```

PATH is an internal command used to extend the DOS search path.

RD Command

```
Syntax: RD [D:]<PATH>
```

RD is an internal command used to erase a subdirectory.

TREE Command

```
Syntax: [D:]TREE [D:] [/F]
```

TREE is an external command used to display the subdirectory structure of a disk.

Hard Disk Commands

BACKUP Command

```
Syntax: [D:][path]BACKUP [Source Drive][path][Filename[.ext]
<Target Drive> [/S] [/M] [/A] [/D] [/F]
```

BACKUP is an external command used to copy hard disk files to formatted floppy diskettes.

FDISK Command

```
FDISK
```

FDISK is an external command used to preformat a disk.

PARK Command

```
Syntax: [D:]PARK
```

PARK is an external command used to move the read/write heads to a vacant cluster just prior to turning off the power.

REPLACE Command

```
Syntax: [D:][Path] REPLACE [Source Drive]<filename<.ext>
<Target Drive> [/S] [/A] [/D] [/P] [/R] [/W]
```

REPLACE is an external command used to update to a new version of DOS. This command is used to copy the new version's external commands and utility programs to the hard disk.

RESTORE Command

```
Syntax: [D:][path]RESTORE <Source Drive> [Target Drive]
[Path][filename[.ext] [/S] [/P] [/M] [/N] [/A] [/B]
```

RESTORE is an external command used to restore files from diskettes created by the BACKUP command to the hard disk.

SYS Command

```
Syntax: [D:][Path]SYS [D:]
```

SYS is an external command used to upgrade your hard disk to a new version of DOS without reformatting the disk.

Filter Commands

FIND Filter

```
Syntax: [D:]FIND "Text" [D:]filename[.ext]
```

FIND is an external command is used to search a file for a specified character string.

MORE Filter

```
Syntax: Command | MORE or [D:]MORE < [D:]filename[.ext]
```

MORE is an external command used to display a full screen of output and then pause until a key is pressed.

SORT Filter

```
Syntax: Command | SORT [/R] [/+N] or [D:]SORT [/R] [/+N]
[D:]filename[.ext]
```

SORT is an external command used to sort information alphabetically.

Batch-File Subcommands

Command	Action
@ECHO	Suppresses display of itself and the following batch file commands. Version 3.3 or later.
ECHO ON/OFF	Toggles on/off the display of batch commands.
ECHO {Text}	Displays messages to the operator.
GOTO	Causes batch-file processing to continue on the line following a specified label.
PAUSE	Temporarily pauses the execution of a batch file.
REM	Documents the batch file.

EDLIN Commands

Command	Function
[n]I	Puts EDLIN into the insert mode and inserts lines of text before line [n].
[n1][,n2]L	Lists lines n1 through n2 on the screen. When n2 is omitted, lines n1 to the end of the file are listed.
[n1][,n2]D	Deletes lines n1 through n2. If n2 is omitted only the line number entered is deleted.
E	Saves the file and returns to DOS.
Q	Returns to DOS without saving the file.
n	Directs Edlin to display a given line and lets you change it.

Error Message Summary

Appendix E

Booting Errors

Problem: Nothing displays on the screen when you do a cold boot.
Solution: Make sure that power is turned on to the monitor and/or the brightness/contrast controls on the monitor are set high enough so that the boot screen can be displayed.

Problem: DOS displays the following message:

```
Non-System or disk error
Replace and strike any key when ready
```

Solution: The disk in drive A is not the DOS disk. Put the DOS disk in drive A and reboot.

Problem: DOS displays one of the following:

```
Invalid date
Enter new date (mm-dd-yy)

or

Invalid time
Enter new time:
```

Solution: You have entered the date or the time incorrectly. Reenter the date or time.

Problem: You have attempted to boot an IBM PC floppy disk computer and DOS displays the following message:

```
The IBM Personal Computer Basic
Version A3.10 Copyright IBM Corp. 1981,1985
61318 bytes free

Ok
```

Solution: You did not place the DOS disk in drive A. Put the DOS disk in drive A and reboot.

CD Error Message

Problem: You entered a CD command and DOS displayed the following message:

```
Invalid Directory
```

Solution: You misspelled the directory name or omitted one or more path symbols.

Changing Drive Error

Problem: You have entered the command C: to change drives to drive C and DOS displays this message:

```
INVALID DRIVE SPECIFICATION
```

Solution: Check the drive specification that you typed and make sure that your microcomputer has a drive C.

COPY Error Messages

Problem: You entered a COPY command and DOS displays the following message:

```
File cannot be copied onto itself
    0 File(s) copied
```

Solution: You have entered a command to copy a file without specify a target drive or filename.

Problem: You entered a COPY command and DOS displays the following message:

```
Insufficient disk space, 0 file(s) copied.
```

Solution: The disk that you are copying to is full. Erase one or more files from the disk or use another disk.

Problem: You entered a COPY command in which a read-only file has been specified as the target file and DOS displays the following message:

```
File creation error
```

Solution: The COPY command will not copy to a read-only file. You must use ATTRIB to change the status of the file.

DISKCOPY Error Message

Problem: You entered a DISKCOPY command and it displays the following message while making the copy:

```
Unrecoverable read error on drive A:
Side 0, track 16
Target diskette may be unusable
```

Solution: You must use the CHKDSK command to check for bad sectors on the source diskette. If the source diskette has bad sectors, DISKCOPY will mark the same sectors on the target diskette as bad sectors. If the source diskette contains bad sectors, you cannot use the DISKCOPY command using that source diskette.

Directory Error Messages

Problem: The DIR command reads the directory of the disk but displays the following message:

```
File not Found
```

Solution: The directory does not contain any files or it contains no filenames that match the wildcard pattern that you specified. Check the wildcard pattern for errors.

Problem: The DIR command is unable to read the directory of the disk in drive A and displays the following message:

```
General Failure error reading drive A
Abort, Retry, Fail?
```

Solution: The disk may not be formatted, or you may be attempting to read a high-density disk in a double-density drive. Check the disk. If it is the correct density for the drive, type R to retry the command, if you receive the same error message, type A to abort the command and return to the system prompt.

Formatting Error Messages

Problem: when the FORMAT command attempts to format a disk, it displays this message:

```
Attempted write-protect violation
Format Failure
Format another (Y/N)?
```

Solution: Check to see if the diskette is correctly inserted in the drive, the disk latch is closed, and the see if the diskette is write-protected. If the diskette is write-protected but you determine that it can be used, change the write-protect status (remove the write-protect tab on a 5.25-inch diskette or close the write-protect window on a 3.5-inch diskette) and attempt to format it again.

184 Error Message Summary

Problem: After the format is complete, DOS displays the following screen:

```
Format Complete

362496 bytes total disk space
  5120 bytes in bad sectors
357376 bytes available on disk
```

Solution: Format the disk again. If DOS still reports bad sectors, the disk is not reliable. If it is a new disk, return it for a refund. If it is not a new disk, discard the disk, because it is not reliable.

Problem: FORMAT displays this message when it attempts to format a diskette:

```
Invalid media or Track 0 bad - disk unusable
Format Failure
Format another
```

Solution: This can be caused by attempting to format high-density diskettes in double-density drives. If you are attempting to format a double-density diskette in a high-density drive, you must use the [/4], or the [/T:80] and [/N:9] options. If these options fail to solve the problem, you have a bad diskette that must be discarded.

General Error Messages

Problem: This error can occur with any command. You entered a command and DOS displayed the following error message:

```
BAD COMMAND OR FILENAME
```

Solution: You misspelled a command or a filename. For example, you enter the DIR command as DI. Check the spelling of the command and/or the filename.

Problem: This error can occur with any command. You entered a command and DOS displayed the following error message:

```
INVALID PARAMETER
```

Solution: You misspelled or omitted a parameter or option. For example, you entered the command DIR/ without specifying an option. Check the command for errors.

MD Error Message

Problem: You entered the MD command and DOS displays the following message:

```
Unable to create directory
```

Solution: The directory already exists or you are trying to create a directory that has the same filename as a file in the root directory. Check to see if the directory exists and, if necessary, use another name.

Printing Error Message

Problem: You have entered the command to print the screen or have toggled on character echo with a <CTRL-P>, and DOS displays the following message:

```
Not ready error writing device PRN
Abort, Retry, Ignore, Fail?
```

Solution: Your microcomputer does not have a printer connected to it, or the printer is not ready to print. If your microcomputer does not have a printer attached, type A to abort the command. If you have a printer attached, make sure that it is ready to print, and then enter R to retry the command. A printer must be turned on, be switched on-line, and have paper in it before it is ready to print.

RD Error Message

Problem: You entered a RD command and DOS displays the following message:

```
Invalid path, not directory,
or directory not empty
```

Solution: RD will only remove a directory that is empty. You must purge the directory of all files and/or subdirectories before you can remove it. If the directory is empty, you must change to some other directory. RD will not remove the current directory.

Redirection Error Message

Problem: You have entered a redirection command and DOS displays the following message:

```
FILE CREATION ERROR
```

Solution: You issued the command without giving DOS a device to redirect the output to. For example, you entered the command DIR > without indicating that PRN should be the device.

REN Error Messages

Problem: You entered a REN command and DOS displays the following message:

```
Invalid parameter
```

Solution: This error is displayed when you specify a target disk drive (for example, REN A:OLDNAME B:NEWNAME). The REN command cannot be used to rename a file on one disk to another disk drive.

Problem: You entered a REN command and DOS displays the following message:

```
Duplicate filename or filename not found
```

Solution: You misspelled the name of the file that you wish to rename, or the new file name already exists. Check the spelling of the old file name and take a directory of the disk to see if the new file name exists.

EDLIN Error Message

*Problem: You are at the EDLIN * prompt and EDLIN displays the following message:*

```
ENTRY ERROR
```

Solution: You attempted to enter a DOS command, for example, CLS, while in the EDLIN program.

Hardware Diagnostics Error Codes

<u>0XX</u>
010 Undetermined problem.
020 Power problem.

<u>1XX</u>
101 Main system board failed.
109 Direct memory access (DMA) test error.
121 Unexpected hardware interrupts occurred.
131 Cassette wrap test failed.
199 User-defined configuration incorrect.

<u>2XX</u>
201 Memory test failed - Displayed in the form of XXXXX YY 201 where XXXXX represents the memory bank and YY represents the actual chip.

<u>3XX</u>
301 Keyboard did not respond to software reset or stuck key failure detected - if stuck key, the key scan code will also be displayed.
302 User-defined error from the keyboard test.

<u>4XX</u>
401 Monochrome memory test, horizontal sync frequency test or video test failed.
432 Parallel port test failed (monochrome adapter).

<u>5XX</u> Color graphics.

<u>6XX</u> Floppy-disk adapter/drives.

<u>9XX</u>
901 Parallel printer port test failed.

<u>10XX</u>
1001 Alternate (lpt2) parallel printer port test failed.

<u>11XX</u>
1101 Asynchoronous serial port (COM1) failed.

<u>12XX</u>
1201 Alternate asynch port (COM2) failed.

<u>13XX</u>
1301 Game controller.
1302 Joystick.

<u>14XX</u>
1401 Graphics printer failed.

Keyboard Diagrams

Appendix F

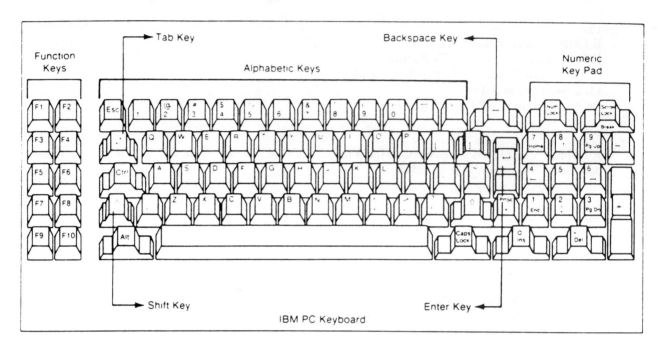

Original Keyboard

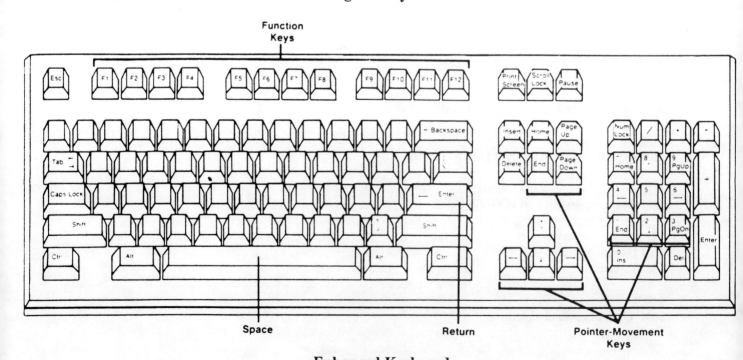

Enhanced Keyboard

Index

-A-

Adapter cards, 4
Alphabetic keyboard, 6
ANSI.SYS, 164
Applications programs, 2
Archive bit, 91
Asterisk (*) wildcard, 66
ATTRIB command, 91
ATTRIB +A parameter, 91
ATTRIB +R parameter, 91
ATTRIB -A parameter, 91
ATTRIB -R parameter, 91
ATTRIB /S (Subdirectory) option, 117
AUTOEXEC.BAT, 15

-B-

<BACKSPACE>, 13
Backslash symbol (\), 19
Backup, 85
BACKUP command, 154
BACKUP /A (Add) option, 155
BACKUP /D (Date) option, 155
BACKUP /M (Modified) option, 155
BACKUP /S (Subdirectory) option, 155
Backup diskettes, 87
Bad sectors, 38
Bank switching, 161
Batch command, 132
Batch file, 132
Bit, 3
Booting, 15
Boot record sector, 38
Bootstrap loader program, 15
BUFFERS directive, 163
BUFFERS directive /X option, 168
Bus, 4
Byte, 3

-C-

<CTRL-BREAK>, 13
<CTRL-C>, 13
<CTRL-P>, 19
<CTRL-S>, 65
CD (Change Directory) command, 18
CD.. command, 112
CD\ command, 112
CHKDSK (CHecK DisK) command, 93
CHKDSK /F (Fix) option, 94
CHKDSK /V (View) option, 93
Cluster, 39
Cold boot, 15
COMMAND.COM, 13
Command driven, 1
COMP (COMPare files), 89
Computer program, 1
CONFIG.SYS, 13
Control keys, 6
COPY command, 85
COPY *.* command, 87
COPY CON:, 133
COPY /V (Verify) option, 87
Current directory, 109
Current drive, 17
Current line, 135
Cursor, 5
Cursor control keys, 6
Cylinder, 39

-D-

D (Delete) EDLIN command, 137
Daisy wheel printer, 8
Data, 2
Data diskette, 40
Data files, 39
Data sectors, 39

DATE command, 17
Default, 14
Default drive, 17
DEL (DELete) command, 90
DEL *.* command, 91
DEL /P (Pause) option, 91
Delimiter, 14
Density, 4
Device drivers, 161
Directives, 161
Directory, 38
DIR /P {Directory Page} option, 66
DIR /W {Directory Wide} option, 66
DIR {DIRectory} command, 65
DIR | SORT, 70
DISKCOMP command, 89
DISKCOPY command, 88
Disk buffer, 163
Disk drive, 2
DOS command, 13
DOS command processor, 13
DOS data structures, 161
DOS editing keys, 68
DOS prompt, 16
DOS shell, 168
DOS system files, 13
DOSSHELL, 168
Dot matrix printer, 8
Dot pitch, 5
DRIVER.SYS, 161

-E-

@ECHO subcommand, 151
<ESC>, 13
E (End) EDLIN command, 138
ECHO OFF, 151
ECHO ON, 151
ECHO subcommand, 151
EDLIN, 133
EMM386.SYS, 169

EMS (Expanded Memory Specification), 161
Enhanced keyboard, 6
Expanded memory, 161
Expansion slot, 4
Extended memory, 161
Extension, 14
External commands, 15

-F-

FDISK command, 154
File Allocation Table (FAT), 38
File name, 14
Filename, 14
Filespec, 14
FILES directive, 162
File specification, 64
Filter commands, 69
Filter symbol, 69
FIND Filter command, 71
FORMAT command, 38
FORMAT /4 option, 42
FORMAT /S option, 41
FORMAT /T:80/N:9 option, 42
FORMAT /V option, 41
Fragmented files, 40
Function keys, 6

-G-

Gigabytes, 161
Global filename characters, 66
GOTO subcommand, 152

-H-

Hardware, 2
Hidden files, 13

-I-

I (Insert) EDLIN command, 136
Ink jet printer, 8
Input buffer, 68
Input redirection operator, 68
Interlaced scanning, 5
Interrupt signal, 65
Internal commands, 15
IO.SYS, 13

-K-

KB, 4
Keyboard, 2
Keyboard Buffer, 6
Kilobytes, 4

-L-

L (List) EDLIN command, 136
LABEL command, 44
Label, 152
Laser printer, 8
LIM (Lotus, Intel, Microsoft), 161
Look-ahead buffer, 168
Lost allocation clusters, 94

-M-

MB, 4
MD {Make Directory} command, 111
Megabytes, 4
Megahertz (MHz), 3
MEM command, 169
Memory chip, 3
Microcomputer, 2
Microcomputer system, 2
Microprocessor chip, 2
Modem, 8
Monitor, 2
MORE filter command, 69
Motherboard, 4
Mouse, 2
MSDOS.SYS, 13

-N-

Noninterlaced scanning, 5
Numeric keypad, 6

-O-

Offset value, 70
Operating system program, 1
Options, 14
Original keyboard, 6
Output redirection operator, 68

-P-

<PAUSE>, 65
<PRINT SCREEN>, 19
Parallel port, 5
Parameters, 14
Parent directory, 109
PARK command, 153
PATH command, 44, 108
Path symbol, 109
Pathname, 110
PAUSE subcommand, 151
Peripheral, 5
Piping, 69
Pixels, 5
Ports, 4
POST (Power On Start Up) program, 15
Printer, 2
Program files, 39
PROMPT command, 18
Protected mode, 161

-Q-

Q (Quit) EDLIN command, 139
Question mark (?) wildcard, 66

-R-

RAM, 3
RAMDRIVE max parameter, 166
RAMDRIVE numfiles option, 165
RAMDRIVE sectorsize option, 165
RAMDRIVE size option, 165
RAMDRIVE /E option, 165
RAMDRIVE.SYS, 164
RD {Remove Directory} command, 113
Read-only file, 91
Redirection, 68
REM subcommand, 140
REN command, 90
REPLACE command, 158
Replaceable parameters, 151
RESTORE command, 157
RESTORE /S (Subdirectory) option, 157
ROM, 3
Root directory, 18

-S-

<SHIFT-PRTSC>, 19
SELECT utility program, 167
Sectors, 38
Serial port, 5
Software, 2
SORT filter command, 70
Subcommands, 140
Subdirectories, 18
Subdirectory system, 108
SYS (SYStem) command, 158
System, 2
System diskette, 41
Systems unit, 2

-T-

Tape backup units, 2
Template, 137
TIME command, 17
Toggle, 6
Tracks, 38
TREE command, 116
TREE /A (ASCII) option, 117
TREE /F (File) option, 116
(TSR) utility programs, 164
TYPE command, 133

-U-

Utility Programs, 2

-V-

Variable marker, 151
Variable name, 151
VDISK.SYS, 164
VER (VERsion) command, 18
Vertical scanning frequency (VSF), 5
VOL (VOLume) command, 44

-W-

Warm boot, 15
Wildcard characters, 66
Word size, 3
Words, 3
Write-protect notch, 42
Write-protect window, 42
Write-protected, 42

-X-

XCOPY command, 87
XCOPY /D (Date) option, 88
XCOPY /E (Empty directory) option, 116
XCOPY /P (Prompt) Option, 88
XCOPY /S, (Subdirectory) option 116
XCOPY /W (Wait) option, 88
XMA2EMS.SYS, 169
XMAEM.SYS, 169